AF147503

ECHOES
of
NALANDA

Dr Kavita A. Sharma is a distinguished scholar and the former president of South Asian University. She taught at Hindu College, Delhi University, for 37 years, serving as its first woman principal. She was also the first woman director of India International Centre. A Fulbright and Shastri Fellow, she has authored several acclaimed books on education and Indian thought, including *Life Is As Is: Teachings from the Mahabharata*. Her pioneering leadership is recognized in the *Limca Book of Records*.

ECHOES
of
NALANDA

KAVITA A. SHARMA

RUPA

Published by
Rupa Publications India Pvt. Ltd 2025
161-B/4, Gulmohar House,
Yusuf Sarai Community Centre,
New Delhi 110049

Sales centres:
Bengaluru Chennai
Hyderabad Kolkata Mumbai

Copyright © Kavita A. Sharma 2025

The views and opinions expressed in this book are the author's own and the facts
are as reported by her; these have been verified to the extent possible, and the
publishers are not in any way liable for the same.

All rights reserved.
No part of this publication may be reproduced, transmitted,
or stored in a retrieval system, in any form or by any means,
electronic, mechanical, photocopying, recording or otherwise,
without the prior permission of the publisher.

P-ISBN: 978-93-6156-958-6
E-ISBN: 978-93-6156-250-1

First impression 2025

10 9 8 7 6 5 4 3 2 1

The moral right of the author has been asserted.

Printed in India

This book is sold subject to the condition that it shall not,
by way of trade or otherwise, be lent, resold, hired out, or otherwise
circulated, without the publisher's prior consent, in any form of
binding or cover other than that in which it is published.

Contents

Foreword

The name Nalanda evokes memories of the great cultural, educational and spiritual institution that served as the premier centre of learning in the East for seven centuries. At its peak, this magnificent university is believed to have accommodated up to a thousand teachers and ten thousand students on its campus. The great Chinese scholars and pilgrims, including Fa-hien, Xuanzang, Yijing and many others, visited this institution, which was established by the Gupta emperors in the early fifth century CE.

However, the path was paved for them by the Indian Buddhist teachers who travelled to China undeterred by the hardships and perils of the journey. Details of their lives and work can only be found in Chinese records. These Indian scholars took with them Buddhist Sanskrit texts and knowledge of Indian astronomy, astrology, music, sculpture and painting—all aspects of Indian culture and civilization. In China, they learnt Chinese and taught Sanskrit. As they gained the favour of the emperors at various times, they established monasteries, study centres and centres for the translation of Buddhist texts into Chinese. They ensured that this civilizational interaction flourished for over a thousand years. This is a remarkable chapter of Indian scholarly achievement that has been forgotten, at least in the public memory. I am glad that Dr Kavita A. Sharma has spoken about it and made it accessible to the public.

The campus of Nalanda University was described in detail by monks and scholars who visited it. It was evidently a magnificent ensemble of *viharas* (monastery) and accommodation for teachers and students that was the pride of Asia. From Nalanda, the teachings of Buddhism spread throughout South and Southeast Asia, including Tibet, China, Korea, Japan and Indonesia. The Chinese scholars brought with them a considerable number of manuscripts that were lost in India and only rediscovered after being translated back into Sanskrit from Chinese. The university was also an important source for the 657 Sanskrit texts brought back by the pilgrim Xuanzang and the 400 Sanskrit texts brought to China by Yijing in the seventh century, which influenced East Asian Buddhism. Many of the texts composed at Nalanda played an important role in the development of Mahayana and Vajrayana Buddhism. Along with Buddhism, Hindu scholars and artisans also travelled to distant lands. Angkor Wat in Cambodia is a marvel of engineering from a thousand years ago. It was initially a Hindu temple and was then built over with Buddhist statues over the centuries.

Unfortunately, Muhammad Bakhtiyar Khalji, in the unfortunate tradition of Muslim invaders and rulers in India for several centuries, sent his troops to Nalanda around 1200 BCE, massacring thousands of students and teachers staying there and destroying the entire campus. It is said that the famous library was so large that it burnt for six months. This tragic event led to the decline of Nalanda. Some of the monks who survived the carnage fled to Tibet, which was why Vajrayana Buddhism flourished there.

Strangely enough, Nalanda was largely forgotten until Alexander Cunnigham, who headed the newly founded Archaeological Survey of India, carried out an official investigation in 1961. Systematic evaluation of the ruins by the Archaeological Survey of India began only in 1950. In 1951, at the suggestion of our first president, Dr Rajendra Prasad, the Nava Nalanda Mahavihara, a modern centre for Pali and Buddhism, was established near the Nalanda ruins and became a deemed university in 2006.

This whole epic of the formidable achievements and final downfall of Nalanda is well described by Dr Kavita A. Sharma in *Echoes of Nalanda*. It is a most welcome and long overdue book for the public, reminding us of one of India's greatest historical achievements. Dr Sharma is well equipped to write this book. Not only does she have a distinguished academic career, she also has a deep and abiding interest in all aspects of education: its history, its evolution over time, and its present structures and systems. This is evident in her work. I congratulate her on her work and recommend the book to all those interested in Nalanda, not only in India but all over the world, especially in South and Southeast Asia.

—Karan Singh
19 August 2022

Preface

When the Government of India established the Nalanda International University in Rajgir in 2010, I wondered what fascination Nalanda held that led to this decision. Rajgir was a rural, underdeveloped place. How could a modern university thrive there? President A.P.J. Abdul Kalam inspired the establishment of the university. Back in 1951, the Nava Nalanda Mahavihara was founded at the behest of the then president, Dr Rajendra Prasad.

The Nalanda Mahavihara drew monastic scholars from various regions, including China, Tibet, Nepal, Indonesia, Korea and Japan. It continues to capture the fascination of many; for instance, a YouTube video recounts how, over 24 years ago, a three-year-old prince from Bhutan insisted on visiting Nalanda, claiming to have been a monk there in a previous life. The China Film Group Corporation, the largest state-owned film production company in China, collaborated with its Indian partner Eros International to produce a noteworthy film titled *Xuanzang* (2016) about the renowned scholar.

I decided to visit Rajgir to experience it firsthand. The journey from Patna was arduous. However, upon arriving at the ancient Mahavihara archaeological site, it felt completely worthwhile. I was overwhelmed by the stunningly beautiful and majestic remnants of the great monastery. It was awe-inspiring. I could only imagine how magnificent the Nalanda Mahavihara must have been during its prime, considering the splendour that remained after fourteen centuries. Yet, only a small portion of the complex has been unearthed.

As I wandered through the ruins of Nalanda, I could almost hear the voices of Chinese scholars like Fa-hien, Xuanzang and I-Ching, along with many others who had traversed miles of inhospitable terrain, risking life and limb, to arrive at Nalanda in search of the authentic Dhamma and the rules for its practice. When the Chinese interaction with Nalanda petered out, numerous Tibetan scholars also began to arrive there. What motivated them to undertake such a dangerous expedition? Perhaps it was the Indian teachers who travelled to China that prepared the ground for this. They spread Buddhism and established centres for the translation of Buddhist texts. I mused that they must have faced similar daunting journeys. The flow of Indian scholars heading to China persisted for centuries, many of them forgotten.

The ruins reverberated with the teachings of the renowned pundits of Nalanda. They not only led lectures but also encouraged their pupils individually in learning and in life. I wondered why so many kings patronized Nalanda—one even travelled from Indonesia. They built impressive viharas here and gifted land to the great monastery. Perhaps their motivations stemmed from Nalanda's status as a wealthy and thriving place at that time. It was culturally vibrant and a bastion of spiritual learning. It was the *karmabhūmi* (field of activity) for both Mahavira and Buddha. The place must have been filled with the echoes of their teachings, and people must have flocked to them.

Nearby sites include the village of Nalaka—the birthplace of Śāriputra—and Uptisya, where Maudgalyayana was born, the Ashoka pillar with its inscription, as well as the ruins of the Nandangarh stupa that is believed to house the Buddha's ashes. And then there's Vaishali, which is said to be the birthplace of Mahavira, while Buddha gave his final sermon in nearby Kolhua. Numerous locations related to the Mahabharata add to the rich tapestry of history. There was so much to see and do, learn and enjoy. These visits kept me busy long after returning home. They inspired me to travel two more times, most recently with my granddaughter Maya. Nalanda and its surroundings speak of a time that can never be replicated.

Rajgir may evolve in line with our notions of a city, teachers and students may impart contemporary knowledge at Nalanda International University, and research may gain momentum at the Nava Nalanda Mahavihara as people worldwide turn to Buddhism in search of peace. However, the inspiring milieu of devotion can never be recreated. It can only be recalled with reverence.

I decided to write *Echoes of Nalanda* to give expression to the voices I heard in my mind as I walked through the sites in Rajgir and nearby areas. This book's journey, much like that of Nalanda, was fraught with difficulties, taking two long years to complete. This was due to the pandemic, which created a backlog at the publishing house. Nevertheless, I am grateful that it will now see the light of day. I truly hope that scholars will be inspired to do further research, especially on Indian scholars who journeyed to China to preach Buddhism, as in India it is important to acknowledge their contributions and bring them to public domain.

Kavita A. Sharma

Introduction

The sight of the ruins of Nalanda, in all their majesty and grandeur, is awe-inspiring. If, after the ravages of time and other depredations over seven centuries, the archaeological remains are so stunning, one can only imagine the unutterable beauty of Nalanda in its heyday. Several questions flash in the mind. Why did the people accept Buddha's teachings? How did he create a *sangha* (monastic order) of the wandering monks? How and why did a *vihara* (monastery) come into being? And how did the vihara become a venerated seat of learning? The names of the monarchs who built and supported Nalanda and honoured its teachers, even when their political fortunes were askew, are emblazoned in the annals of Nalanda Mahavihara, now in ruins. Why did notable Chinese scholars like Fa-hien, Xuanzang and I-Ching come to Nalanda, braving perilous journeys? This could not have happened in a vacuum. Something must have paved the way for them to resolve to leave their hearths and homes, their sanctuaries, to come to this far-off place.

Was it the routes established by traders who carried more than just trade goods? They also brought along customs, religions, knowledge and traditions with them. Was it the influence of Indian Buddhist scholars who travelled to China preaching the Buddha's Dhamma (Dharma in Sanskrit), establishing translation centres of Buddhist texts? Remarkably, these Indian scholars learnt Chinese and taught Sanskrit to the Chinese to form translation teams. What did scholars like Xuanzang and I-Ching learn in Nalanda? What was so special about Nalanda that it attracted students and scholars from places far and wide? They came from China, Central Asia, Korea and Tibet, to name just a few. The ruins whisper of a bygone way of life, discipline and devotion that is difficult to replicate, though still worth striving for. Why did such a famous seat of learning decline, and when was it destroyed? Perhaps its beauty and splendour, fame and renown became its eventual undoing, paving the way for its destruction.

As one ruminates over Nalanda, one realizes it was the culmination of one man's vision—his *tapasya* (penance). His forward-looking thought process, egalitarian outlook and enlightenment shook the world, the impact of which is still felt across places in different ways. While it is unnecessary to go into details about the life of the Buddha and the teachings and concepts of Buddhism as we know them today, a glimpse of these makes one understand why they fostered the tremendous spiritual and intellectual activity that eventually led to the founding of monasteries and finally the establishment of the Nalanda Mahavihara.

The Life of Buddha and the Coming of Buddhism

When Gautam Buddha rejected a life of luxury and pleasure to seek the truth, he was not doing anything unique. Wandering almsmen had always been a part of India's landscape. What was exceptional was what this forsaking of worldly life meant to the Buddha—not a step into solitude or a plunge into a social vacuum, but a transition from one condition of life to another, from home to homelessness. Homelessness did not mean a state of isolation, seclusion, or lack of companionship. A monk could choose to go to the forest, as stated in the *Vanapattha Sutta*, but he was not obliged. He was usually seen as part of a community, a village or a township. What was important was that he cultivated his spiritual life in complete awareness of his human frailties, irrespective of where he lived. Hence, a layperson could aspire to this transition to homelessness just as much as a monk.

What was the Buddha's Dhamma, and how did it differ from others? The *Brahmajala Sutta* emphasises that the Buddha was not a preacher of the arbitrary, like the other sect leaders of speculative systems. His Dhamma was about what he had realized and experienced. It was not given to a particular sect but meant for humankind. Several statements have been attributed to the Buddha on various occasions, emphasising the universality of his character as a teacher of religion. He is presented not only as *sattha*, the authoritative teacher of his sect, but also as *sammasambuddha* (Supreme Buddha) or universal teacher, indicating the universal character of his Dhamma.

The Buddha realized that the 'truth' he had received or attained had a dynamic quality that had to be transformed into a message, as it would not find fruition or fulfilment as a static form of knowledge. This 'truth' could not be known to anyone except the one who cognized it—'The Buddha understood Buddhism.' He named it the *amatta* (deathless) when he turned it into a message and moulded it into a Dhamma to bring it into the purview of average human understanding.

For the Buddha, truth meant the alleviation of suffering through self-knowledge, self-culture and self-control, without any extremes—following the Middle Path. Incredibly, when he sought out people to tell them what he had learned about his own experience through meditation, he could only think of the five ascetics who had previously abandoned him when he rejected austerities after realizing that the modification of the body could not be the route to enlightenment.

Although they had left him before, they became his followers again when they heard what he had to say. They were the first *bhikkus*, the ordained male monastics of the Buddha. The simplicity of what the Buddha said was revolutionary. He did not discuss God, the soul, the afterlife, or other such abstruse concepts. All he said was, 'I teach one thing and one thing only—suffering and the end of suffering.' This is the core of Buddhist thought that has since been expanded across numerous volumes. The Buddha summarized it into the Four Noble Truths—the existence of suffering, the cause of suffering, the ways to end the cause of suffering, and the path to the end of suffering. What is this path about? It is undoubtedly not about extreme indulgence or self-mortification. In his first sermon, Buddha said:

> Monks, these two extremes should not be practised by one who has left the household life. (What are the two?) There is the addiction to indulgence of sense pleasures, which is low, common, the way of ordinary people, unworthy and unprofitable; and there is the addiction to self-mortification, which is painful, unworthy, and unprofitable.

Avoiding these two extremes, the *Tathagata* (the Perfect One) has realized the Middle Path: He gives vision and knowledge and leads to calm, insight, enlightenment and *nibbana* (nirvana). What was the Middle Path realized by the Tathagata? It is the Noble Eightfold Path—right view, right thought, right speech, right action, right livelihood, right effort, right mindfulness and right concentration.[1]

At the centre of the Buddha's Dhamma was, therefore, the human being and his relationship to others and his life on earth. The path of the Buddha (he also referred to himself as Tathagata) was not that of a recluse, for that was only an escape. He expounded on the path his followers must take, that of right mindfulness, effort and concentration, and the ascetics duly accepted his teachings. They felt that they had found a reformer in him—one who was brimming with an earnest sense of moral purpose and at the same time, abreast with contemporary intellectual culture. He was a man who had the originality and courage to put forth his

---

[1] 'Dhammacakkappavattana Sutta: Setting in Motion the Wheel of Truth', Piyadassi Thera (trans.), *Access to Insight*, BCBS Edition, 30 November 2013, https://tinyurl.com/buddhist-studies. Accessed on 23 January 2025.

mind and experience, with the awareness of opposing views, and espoused a doctrine which said that salvation could be found in this life through an inward change wrought by self-culture and self-control.

Teaching was inherent in the Buddha's way of life. He taught and asked his monks to teach in a language that people could understand. Since the Buddha spoke about what he had personally learnt through experimentation and experience and not from any holy texts, it rang true. He gave directions to people, stimulated their minds and dispelled their doubts. For forty-five years, he relentlessly taught anyone and everyone, regardless of their social standing, caste, creed or gender. Even in his last moments, he asked his monks if they had any doubts they needed to clarify, as he did not want them to regret not asking him about something they wished to be enlightened about, but they did not. His last message was that they should be a light unto themselves and not depend on anyone else.

Following the Buddha meant the monks had to constantly interact with each other and the larger community. Passages from the early scriptures show that the faith and message delivered to the disciples and the first monk-followers was not regarded as a 'system' but as a way of life or a form of self-culture—a Dhamma whereby one could escape all the sorrows that arise from the life of the world and the flesh. It is described as *magga*—the path to the cessation of suffering— and those to whom the way has been opened are the initiates, the ordained, the 'knowledgeable'; they are then enjoined to extend this knowledge to the *bahujan*, or people at large. The religion must become *bahujannin* or that of the people. And so, Buddhism thrived and spread in India as a bahujan religion and was not primarily characterized by the practice of monkhood or the formation of an exclusive sect. If his followers formed a sect, the Buddha believed that this should not be seen as an end but as a means to promote the welfare and happiness of many. This was the gist of his exhortation to his monks when they had grown into a body fit to take up his mission.

Formation of the Bhikku Sangha

Who are the bhikkus? And how did they form a sangha, a monastic order? A bhikku is an almsman. The bhikku differs from an ordinary beggar in the sacramental character of his begging. His begging is not just a means of subsistence but an outward token that signifies he has renounced the world and all its goods and thrown himself into a sparse existence, living on the chance of public charity. He has renounced worldly life and joined the contemplative mendicant community.

The nucleus of a bhikku sangha, or collective of bhikkus, was laid when the five ascetics to whom the Buddha preached his first sermon became his monk-followers. Soon, a group of disciples received ordination at his hands and joined the Order of the Master or the Buddha. Legends of the Theravada canon tell the story of the early growth of this body of disciples. Initially, they formed a cult group that recognized the Buddha as their lord and master and accepted his given system as Dhamma. They formed a union of faith with the Buddha as their master. As others joined and the union grew, the Buddha entrusted the disciples with a mission. They were to go forth and wander for the good of the people, with compassion for the world. When they received this message from the Buddha, the group was not even a 100 strong and very few were capable of the task at hand. The canon says that only 61 *arhat*s (those who gained insight) lived in the world then.

To outsiders, this group was known as the ordained followers of *Shakyaputta* or the Buddha, but the group simply called itself the bhikku sangha. They looked up to the Buddha as their sattha and their allegiance to him unified them as a collective. The initial primitive sangha, a small body of *Shakyaputtiya shramanas* (wandering monks or seekers), gradually transformed from a wandering sect to a sacred order. This was mainly due to the monks' retreat during the rainy season when they stayed together in groups.

Vassa: The Rain Retreat

The seeds of transformation are found in the rain retreat. The rule that the wanderer must suspend his wandering and remain in retreat during the season of rains is among the canonical regulations of different sects. The Buddhists refer to this retreat as *vassa*. According to the *Mahavagga*, one of the principal holy texts in Buddhism, people were irked that the shramanas travelled through the seasons, harming vegetation. When the bhikkus informed the Blessed One of this, he prescribed they abstain from travelling in the rainy season. The Blessed One then dwelt in Rajagriha (present-day Rajgir), in Kalandakanivapa, and the retreat during the rainy season had not yet been instituted by the Blessed One for the bhikkus. Thus, the bhikkus went on their travels during winter, summer, and the rainy season alike.

People were annoyed—'How could the Shakyaputtiya shramanas continue their travels alike during winter, summer, and the rainy season?' They asked whether the ascetics who belonged to the Titthiya school, whose doctrine was ill-preached during the rainy season, did not retire during that time and arrange places for themselves to live in. Thus, they objected that the Shakyaputtiya shramanas continued to travel across winter, summer and the rainy season, crushing the green herbs and vegetables and destroying the lives of many small things.

Some bhikkus heard that the people were annoyed and told the Blessed One about this. Consequently, the Blessed One, after delivering a religious discourse, thus addressed the bhikkus, 'I prescribe, O bhikkus, that you enter upon vassa.'[2] However, the

---

[2]Davids, Thomas William Rhys, *The Mahavagga*, Jazzybee Verlag, Germany, 2012, p. 229.

Buddhist vassa evolved differently from the rain retreat of the other sects, as it became an opportunity for the bhikkus to live in the congregation. They were not expected to live anywhere or alone and companionless, but to settle in a congregation of fellow monks. Thus, a settlement of monks came up with its boundaries, allowing the bhikkus to live together without intrusion. Being almsmen, they naturally made their vassa settlements in localities where alms were available. However, some preferred to live in forest clearings and were called *arannaka*s or forest dwellers.

The bhikku settlements were in towns and villages. The accommodation problem, however, for the rain retreat was not the same in the villages as in the cities. In a village, the first task of the bhikkus was to demarcate the boundaries and build their shelters within these. In a town or a city, a wealthy lay devotee may be found who would be inclined to donate his private garden to the bhikkus for their period of vassa, or even permanently. Thus, two types of rain retreats emerged—those in the villages were called *avasa*, and those in or near towns or cities were called *arama*. While the avasas were built and maintained by the monks, the aramas had private enclosures and were looked after by the donors.

Although the retreat lasted only three months, it had a profound and lasting impact, reflected in institutions, customs and practices reminiscent of the congregational character. Several ceremonies were instituted. One of these was the recital of a *Patimokkha*—a set of 227 monastic rules, literally meaning 'that which is binding'— which later developed into a congregational service. Then, there were ceremonies like the *pavarana* (an invitation to stay at the vassa) and *kathina* (the distribution of robes for the new year commencing after the vassa). Originally, a Patimokkha was the congregational chanting of the confession of faith by assembled bhikkus. Held only once in six years, it essentially comprised summing up the fundamental injunctions of the religion. It was probably prevalent among the bhikkus since the early days of the sangha. Over time, it morphed into a recital of a code of offences against the rules and regiments of monastic life and was held fortnightly.

As donations started coming in liberally for the upkeep of the monks, wandering for alms lost much of its urgency and compulsion. Gradually, the vassa settlements began to turn into domiciles. The monks themselves were aware of this. Although the life of wandering was not immediately given up, a new custom began to take root whereby monks returned to and inhabited the avasa and arama of their last rain retreat. Those who habitually lived together in one avasa during their vassa began to be distinguished from those who lived in another. This impacted how accommodation was allocated and acquired for and during the vassa.

Each vassa began to have a company of old residents and newcomers who would turn up to occupy one of these abodes. As space was limited, preference was given to co-dwellers or those who had cohabited for the last vassa, and an ad hoc chamberlain was appointed to allot seats and bedding for the incoming monks. The rules for this allotment were a step toward turning the retreat shelters into residential units. Three separate times were fixed for the allotment of lodgings: the earlier, the later and the intervening. The first was on the day following the full moon of *Ashadha* (June–July), the second was later in the month following the next full moon, and the third was on the day following *Pavarana*, marking the end of the three lunar months of vassa. The third allotment was *Autarmukutta*, which involved giving up the claim to the bedding and seats during non-vassa. This is contradictory as the avasa was not supposed to be occupied during non-vassa, so fresh allotment of bedding and seats at the end of a vassa should be meaningless. But this indicates that many monks chose to remain in the avasa beyond the vassa—the rule of the three-month vassa was in decline. Thus, the monks staying at a particular avasa emerged as a new social unit.

Vihara

An arama or an avasa at this stage of development was not an organized monastery but only a colony of monks. It was so circumscribed by its limits that it was wholly independent and unitary. The transition from wandering to a settled life was gradual. Within the boundaries of an avasa were huts for the monks, and the place came to be called a vihara. Over time, the vihara became synonymous with the monastery. A single monk or a group of monks could occupy a vihara. The portion allotted to each monk for his stay was called *parivena*. It only had provision for a bed and a seat with furniture of the simplest kind.

Sangharama

An arama denoted a pleasure ground, usually belonging to a well-to-do citizen in a city or suburb, laid out as an orchard or flower garden. When the owner gave it permanently to the monks, it was called a *sangharama* or arama owned by a sangha. Over time, it simply became a large monastery. The donor of an arama not only gave his property to the sangha but also continued to look after it, erecting new buildings to meet the needs of the monks and keeping the space clean and habitable. He could employ a staff of servants and superintendents for this purpose. It is said that when King Bimbisara of Magadha obtained the Buddha's permission to employ servants in a sangharama, many of them filled an entire village. The sangharama was always amply stocked with provisions.

As bhikkus came together in sangharamas, they needed a permanent meeting hall because certain ceremonies, such as the *uposatha*, had to be observed. Initially, the uposatha, derived from the Sanskrit word *paratha*, was a special day of prayer and meditation to purify the defiled mind, leading to inner calm and joy. It was also a day of reciprocity between the monastics and the common people. It was a day when the monks re-emphasised their communal commitments while the laypeople made a conscious effort to practise Buddha's precepts and meditate. The ceremony was held in the monks' cells in succession, but the recital of prayers had to be abbreviated because of the exigencies of space, making it impossible for all the resident monks to attend. Even the entire vihara could not accommodate all the monks.

Consequently, an artificial limit, called *uposathaparamukka*, was adopted, making the service valid only until it could be correctly heard. The vihara temporarily arranged for an *uposathagarra* service, and was swept, cleaned and provided with lights for the occasion. Therefore, a suitably large common meeting hall was needed. However, building such a meeting hall with the proper interior decor was a task too difficult for the monks to shoulder by themselves. Help was expected from wealthy devotees who deemed it an act of exceptional merit to build such a hall and give it permanently to the sangha.

Jivikarama was one such *arama*, which Jivika, a well-known physician and one of the wealthiest and most sincerely devoted followers of the Buddha, gave him. He presented his great orchard of mango trees on the outskirts of Rajagriha, a short distance from the foot of the Gridhrakuta Mountain, which was the Buddha's favourite resort when he sojourned there. Another similar place was Jetavana, which was continuously occupied till the last days of Buddhism. When Fa-hien (originally Sehi) visited Jetavanarama in the early fifth century CE, a vihara stood there. But when Xuanzang (originally Pen Yi), the second Chinese monk-scholar and the most famous of them all, visited Jetavanarama in 636 CE, it did not exist. He wrote, 'Tradition says [...] there were ninety sangharamas surrounding the Jetavana chapel, all of which, with one exception, were occupied by priests.'[3]

---

[3]Xuanzang, *Si-yu-ki: Buddhist Records of the Western World*, Samuel Beal (trans.),

There used to be a sangharama there, but now everything is in ruins. The residences are wholly destroyed; only the foundations remain, except for a solitary brick building, standing alone amidst the ruins, containing an image of the Buddha. Yet, this site does not seem to have been abandoned. Another vihara, not too modest in scale, was built here at an unknown date after Xuanzang's visit. As late as 1130 CE, it received a charter from Varanasi under the seal of King Govindachandra of Kannauj. He gifted six villages to the sangharama, whose chief, Buddhabhattarak, lived in the great monastery of Jetavanarama.

The Buddhists' Order

With the emergence of collective life, Dhamma expanded to Dhamma-Vinaya. Translated as 'doctrine and discipline', it could mean rules for the religious system. Recognizing *Vinaya* as part of Dhamma marks the first step in the transition of the Buddhists from a sect to an order. The primary intent and purpose of the code was to unite the sangha on a new basis. Earlier, the cementing bond was only the Dhamma and the sangha's affirmation and confession of faith in it. As the sangha evolved, it recognized and accepted appropriate rules and standards of living for the monks. As the comprehensive body of rules based on agreement and convention grew, the task to organize, edit and classify them was taken up, making them not a mere manual of regulations but the corpus of laws that derived their authority from the Buddha himself.

Because of its system of laws, the sangha became a social unit claiming protection and sovereignty. The only story of the persecution of Buddhist monks by an Indian ruler is that of Pushyamitra, although little is known about his real motive. He was a general of the Maurya Empire in 185 BCE, who supposedly

---

Routledge, California, 2008, p. xlviii.

assassinated the last Mauryan emperor, Brihadratha Maurya, and proclaimed himself emperor. He is said to have cruelly persecuted Buddhist monks, although there is controversy about the veracity of this claim. However, Taranath states, 'Then the *brāhmaṇa* king *Pusyamitra, along with other *tīrthika-s* (non-believers), started war, and thus, burnt down numerous monasteries from the madhya-deśa to *Jalandhara. They also killed many vastly learned monks. But most of them fled to other countries.'[4] It should be noted that many modern scholars have not accepted the claim that Pushyamitra was a persecutor of Buddhists.

Apart from its effect on moulding sangha life, the Vinaya ensured protection from violent powers. Once created, a monk establishment would continue to exist for centuries unless deserted by the monks, decayed to dilapidation, or demolished internally or by foreign invaders. The Vinaya was also formulated to achieve an internal unity of a sangha through several features, like the system of joint deliberation, the postulation of equality of all members in decision-making on matters of common concern, the rule of the majority, the rejection of personal dictation, and the like.

This *samagatta* (the entirety of sangha) performed a *sanghakamma* (an action that impacted the sangha as a whole). The process of sanghakamma was jealously guarded and strictly insisted upon. One safeguard against the degeneration of the sangha is said to be the transaction of all sanghakamma in a valid manner, that is, in concord and full assembly. All qualified inmates of a sangharama had to be assembled. Those disqualified were nuns, male or female novices, and those labouring under any of the 24 disabilities listed in the *Mahavagga*. If a monk could not join the assembly for any reason, he had to remain outside its boundary or send a proxy to convey his consent.

---

[4]Taranatha, *History of Buddhism in India*, Lama Champa and Alaka Chattopadhyaya (trans.), Motilal Banarsidass Publishers, Delhi, 2018, p. 121.

As the followers grew in number, a settled rather than a wandering life became the norm. The original sangha split into many delimited and autonomous groups. Each of them was now a sangha, and although the original concept of the sangha became a mere idea, it was never entirely given up. At this point, rules became necessary to regulate the incoming and outgoing monks to prevent disruptions. These are found in the *Cullavagga*—the journal of Buddhist ethics. These rules also ensured proper conduct and good relations between the old residents and newcomers.

Development of Settlements

The development of monastic settlements led to the institution of practices that were not conducive to a dispersed way of living.

The first practice was a system of training called *Nyssa*, which involved dependence on a teacher and a probationary period of usually ten years between the calling and full ordination.

The second practice that developed involved the monks holding symposia and debates. This was called *Abhidhamma Katha*, from which the ancient Buddhist texts evolved, such as *Abhidhamma* (*Abhidharma* in Sanskrit).

The third practice was performing collective rites and ceremonies, such as uposatha, Patimokkha, *pavarna* and kathina, which already existed and could only be maintained regularly in a collective.

The *upathana shala*, or meeting hall, symbolized the collective, congregational life. As the sangha developed, a transition occurred from the older type of settlements in avasa or arama to *lena* or a compact, unitary establishment for a settled body of monks, enabling it to function undisturbed as a sovereign body—a sangha by itself. Without completely barring outsiders, it was a proper monastery specifically meant for the residents of a single sangha.

Fa-hien's description of the Hinayanist monasteries he visited in Udyana, on India's northwestern border, illustrates the nature of the settlement. If a strange bhikku arrived here, they entertained him for three days. At the end of the three days, they bade him seek a permanent place to rest. Lenas grew into viharas. In the older literature, a vihara was a dwelling place or the private apartment of a single bhikku. When it later developed into a communal dwelling of more generous proportions, private apartments were constructed within it, called *parivenas*, which were living quarters within a lena.

A vihara could be defined as a kind of lena with communal dwelling. Earlier, when a vihara was built by the *Setthi* of Rajagriha, for example, it was just shacks for the bhikkus as shelters from the rain. Each shack was so small and flimsy that 60 shacks could be put up in one day. Over time, a vihara developed into a dwelling house for a company of monks. The communal vihara was styled as a lena to distinguish it from avasa or arama. It was private in that it was built to house a single monk fraternity, with reservations and discriminations regarding *senasana* or who could dwell here. It was not intended to receive bhikkus from all quarters. Lenas were extensive settlements that marked a shift within the monastic community from small settlements to monasteries.

Since teaching and learning are an essential part of Buddhism, it was a natural progression for a cluster of monasteries to form a *mahavihara*. One of the most important of these monasteries was the Nalanda Mahavihara, a sacred place of learning located not too far from Rajagriha or Pataliputra.

Unravelling the History of Nalanda

The history of Nalanda can only be pieced together from the records of the Chinese monks and the last Tibetan monk who came to the university. The records of the journeys and stays of visitors from other parts of the world, if any, are not available, at least in English. Many Chinese monks came to India and perhaps to Nalanda, but only three, Fa-hien, Xuanzang and I-Ching, left detailed records that form the backbone of the knowledge about Nalanda. Others, such as Sung-yun, left sketchy records, while many others left none. The names of 180 Chinese monks who came to India have come to light, and I-Ching has written brief accounts of 56 of them. The travails of their journeys, the places they passed through, and their experiences are encapsulated in the records of these three celebrated Chinese monks. From around the eighth century, monks from Tibet started pouring in, and some of their writings and records are also available. The Indian monks did not keep any records of their travels or stays in China and Tibet. Their histories have been gleaned from the records found in these countries. However, Indian monks and scholars paved the way for Chinese monk scholars to come to India. They must have done phenomenal work for the Chinese to undertake such a hazardous journey.

Indian Buddhist scholar-monks visited China around the first century CE, carrying their knowledge from an oral tradition. They must have experienced the same deprivations and hazards that the Chinese and Tibetan monks referred to in their writings. Although they were at the forefront of establishing Buddhism in China, setting up monasteries and spearheading the translations of Buddhist texts, no records of their sojourns have been found in India. They would have had to learn the Chinese language and teach Sanskrit to the Chinese. This must have required tremendous dedication. Why did they not write accounts of their experiences? Probably because they came from an oral tradition of passing on knowledge, which was not the case with the Chinese. This was the cultural difference between the two civilizations. Even today in India, the oral tradition holds sway when studying classical languages or even the arts.

The travel between China and India speaks of the romance of the Silk Road, which was actually a conglomeration of many trade routes that enabled the exchange of goods and culture between two ancient civilizations.

As Liang Chi Chao, the then president of the erstwhile Universities Association in Peking, said in his welcome note to Tagore when he visited China in 1924:

> What we as historians are able to vouch for is that the first communication between us as brothers occurred in the first century of the era of Christ. From the tenth year of Han Yung Tsin to the fifth year of Tang Chen Yuan (67–789 AD), roughly spanning 800 years, the Hindu scholars who came to China numbering twenty-four, to which may be added thirteen from Kashmir (which in Tang times was not recognized as part of India) thus making thirty-seven in all, not counting those who came from other countries on the eastern and western sides of Chung Lin (Turkestan). Our scholars who went to India to study during the period from the western Tsin to the Tang dynasties (265–790 AD) numbered 187, the names of 105 of whom we can ascertain. Among the most famous from India were all Tamolosa (Dharma-raksha), Chu Shien (Buddha-bhadra), and Chen Ti (Jina-bhadra) and from China, Fa Hien, Yuan Chuang and I Tsing.[5]

The travelogues of Fa-hien, the first Chinese Buddhist monk to visit India, are interlaced with too many romanticized notions to be deciphered accurately. Nonetheless, they provide a noteworthy account of Magadha. Around 400 CE, though Nalanda Mahavihara did not exist, the Magadha region was a prosperous seat of socioreligious learning—it was the *karmabhumi* (land of working out the karma) for both Mahavira and the Buddha. Scholars like Nagarjuna and Aryadeva taught here, and King Ashoka's stupas and edicts dotted the landscape.

---

[5]Tagore, Rabindranath, *Talks in China*, Rupa Publications, New Delhi, December 2002.

Almost three centuries passed before Xuanzang journeyed to India and—at the behest of his emperor—left a detailed and seemingly accurate account that Sir Alexander Cunningham, the Founder Director-General of the Archaeological Survey of India, used for his excavations in the nineteenth century. From Xuanzang we learn about the establishment and growth of Nalanda under the patronage of a galaxy of mighty kings. Xuanzang's fame resounded both in India and China as an outstanding scholar. On his return to China, he established a regular school of translation and the methodology of translation under royal patronage. The king and the crown prince themselves wrote the prefaces to the works produced under his leadership. Finally, I-Ching, who spent ten years at Nalanda, wrote a detailed account of life at the university, elucidating the factors—discipline, dedication and a constant striving for perfection of body and mind—that enabled the place to thrive.

Yet, if Nalanda was such a great seat of learning that survived for eight centuries, what caused its eventual decline? Perhaps there was an inherent contradiction between Buddhism as a religion of the people and the elitism of a Mahavihara like Nalanda, just as there was between the ideal of minimal possession prescribed for the monks and the prosperity of the university through the plentiful land grants and management of estates donated for the same. Then there was the conflict between the austere teachings of the Buddha, born out of the experience of suffering and the desire to alleviate that in others, as opposed to the complex Sanskrit texts and elaborate ritualism of Mahayana and Tantrism that developed at Nalanda. One wonders whether the Buddha predicted this decline, given that he was born a prince and was aware of existing societal tensions. He was himself attacked on these grounds despite renouncing his kingdom, and could perhaps imagine a time when his Dhamma would decline and wars would ensue. One also wonders about the wheel of time and the socio-political and cultural changes it begets to make an institution like Nalanda untenable. Above and beyond all this, Buddha's perspicacity comes to mind. The longing to recreate this bygone era of radical enlightenment perhaps resides in most of us. But can it be done?

1

The Interactions between Two Civilizations

The magnificent remains of the Nalanda Mahavihara not only tell the story of Nalanda as a seat of learning but also bear witness to 2,000 years of cultural and material exchange between India and China, as travellers from diverse backgrounds went back and forth on foot or horseback, traversing some of the most challenging terrains. Of course, as historians Tansen Sen and Wang Gungwu point out, the historical exchanges do not inevitably imply a connection between the nations of India and China, as these two entities did not exist in their current forms before the 1940s. Many people who are now a part of the two countries had distinct political and cultural identities and pursued their independent external relationships, not belonging to a single country. Therefore, as Tan Chung (an authority on Chinese history) stated, the interactions between India and China were between two civilizations and not between two nation-states. Also intimately interwoven with them were connections with people living in several other regions, including locations outside Asia.

Physical Terrain

The key regions between India and China were the spaces occupied by the Himalayan range, the Taklamakan Desert, the mountainous terrain of Burma (now Myanmar), and the maritime regions of the Bay of Bengal and the South China Sea. The expansive network of trade routes stretched across regions of present-day Afghanistan, Iran, Russia, the Arabian Peninsula and the Levant. Mountain ranges, deserts, seas and steppes influenced the growth of the corridors of movement. Most westward trade from China passed through the Hexi Corridor—a chain of oases passing through the Gansu province in present-day China, flanked by the Gobi Desert and the Tian Mountains. The corridor opened into the Tarim Basin and eventually into the Taklamakan Desert in present-day Xinjiang. Located north of the Tibetan Plateau, between the Kunlun and the Tian mountain ranges, this enormous desert contained a few oases around which influential cities and kingdoms grew. Travellers either went across the Pamir Mountains through the Torugary Pass to Samarkand or the Hindu Kush via the Khyber Pass to Purushapura and further south to India. Bactria was nestled between the Pamir and the Hindu Kush, straddling modern-day Afghanistan, Tajikistan and Uzbekistan. The corridor played a vital role in the history of what came to be known as the Silk Road. To its west, Persia lay between the Caspian Sea and the Arabian Sea. Still further west was the Arabian Peninsula, the Levant and the Mediterranean Sea.

Silk Road across Dynasties

The nineteenth-century German geographer Ferdinand von Richthofen coined the term Silk Road in his multi-volume geographical history of China. He named it after the routes along which Chinese silk moved from the Han Empire (206 BCE–220 CE) to Central Asia, from which the Han learned about Western geography. The term captured the popular imagination, inspiring films, novels and even tour packages, although it was not just a road but a term for diverse trade routes.

The earliest movement on the Silk Road was due to the demand for luxury goods like silk among the elites of the nomadic tribes to the north of China and of the Chinese empire. The nomadic tribes constantly troubled China and dealing with them inspired some of the early attempts to make contact with India.

The Chinese Empire was surrounded to the east, south and west by the natural boundaries of the Pacific Ocean, the Himalayas, and the expanse of the Gobi Desert. The external threat originated in the open north, from a strong military power called the Xiongnu. This poor, primitive nomadic community had a warlike culture aided by a strong, swift cavalry. The Xiongnu would invade northern China whenever it had enough resources, and China could never cope with such an aggressor. The Xiongnu strategy was not to seriously fight the Chinese expeditionary force during the latter's advance. Instead, when the Chinese forces began to withdraw, as their food supplies dwindled, they launched a fierce attack, leading to numerous Chinese casualties.

Between the seventh century BCE and the first century CE, the relations of the Chinese imperial court with its nomadic neighbours set the foundation for the growth of trans-Eurasian trade. After their former rivals, the Yuezhi (ancient nomadic pastoralists), migrated into Central Asia in the second century BCE, the Xiongnu became a dominant power in the steppe of northeastern Central Asia, centred on an area that would later become Mongolia. The Xiongnu were also active in areas that are now part of Siberia, Inner Mongolia, Gansu and Xinjiang. Their relations with adjacent Chinese dynasties to the southeast were complex, with repeated periods of conflict and intrigue alternating with tributes, trade and marriage treaties. Notably, Qin Shi Huang, the first emperor of Qin and founder of the Qin Dynasty, built the Great Wall, which was extended and fortified during the later Han dynasties, to stop the incursion of the Xiongnu.

The rise of the Qin state began with King Mu of Qin, who ruled between 659 and 624 BCE. He distinguished himself as the strongman of the Eastern Zhou Confederation during spring and autumn in competition with King Huan of Qi (reigned 685–643 BCE),

King Xiang of Song (reigned 650–637 BCE), King Wen of Jin (reigned 636–628 BCE) and King Zhuang of Chu (reigned 613–591 BCE). Later, an outstanding administrator named Shang Yang (390–338 BCE) arose in the state of Qin, who initiated reforms based on the idea that the state becomes strong when influential people are weak, and vice versa. He wanted to stop the unruly behaviour of the dominant groups in society and strengthen the state. In the meantime, he encouraged ordinary people to increase production. He protected the interests of farmers while restricting merchants from profiteering. All this made Qin prosperous and powerful. The Qin state was the dark horse among the warring states in China, and Qin Shi Huang (259–210 BCE), who had become the king of Qin at the age of 13 and Emperor of China at 39, led from the front.

The emperor's conquest went beyond the pre-Qin borders of China. After vanquishing the southernmost Chu state, he annexed a large area of the Yangtze valley into his domain. In 218 BCE, he conquered present-day Guangdong and Guangxi. During 214–213 BCE, the emperor sent troops to fight the Xiongnu, who harassed China from its northern border. He then had the Great Wall built to prevent any swift incursion into North China by Xiongnu horsemen. The Qin Emperor made Xianyang (Shaanxi province) the capital of China.

After the emperor died, his son and successor was overthrown after only three years of rule. The descendants of the rulers of the erstwhile states vanquished by Qin saw an opportunity to return to the pre-Qin order. The Han Dynasty was the successor to the Qin Dynasty and inherited its political structure. However, it learned from its predecessor and eased all repressive measures against the people, consolidating and unifying China. It established a new capital in Chang'an (Xian), keeping China's political centre in the western part of the country.

Emperor Wen presided over the Han Dynasty's transition from infancy to adulthood. China was fortunate to have a ruler like Wen during this transitional period because he cared about the country's vitality and people's livelihoods. Letting the people live in peace, the emperor implemented the ancient Chinese philosopher Laozi's idea of quietude as part of his governing philosophy, leading to an orderly society. The reigns of Emperors Wen and Jing, totalling about 50 years, can be regarded as the most genteel and population-friendly period in Chinese history. Han Emperor Jing was succeeded by his son Liu Che (157–87 BCE), who reigned for 53 years (141–87 BCE). He was the outstanding, world-famous Han Emperor Wu, who firmly established Confucian teaching for China's development with the help of a prominent scholar, Dong Zhongshu.

According to Tan Chung, of all Han rulers, Wu probably has the most legends in China relating to the Indian visitors he received.[6] According to one of them, an Indian visitor presented him with some trappings for horses adorned with marvellous jewels. At night, these jewels shone, filling the room with light just as in the daytime. Another story is about resurrection fumigation, which is taken seriously in Chinese literature and by traditional pharmacologists. The story goes that an Indian emissary came to meet Emperor Wu during a severe epidemic in the Han capital, Chang'an. He presented the emperor with an egg-shaped perfume, which he burnt on the advice of the Indian presenter, whereupon those who had died due to the epidemic came back to life.

These two stories should not be dismissed casually. Ancient India was famous for jewellery and perfume, therefore such gifts during the 53-year reign of Emperor Wu (141–87 BCE) may not be hearsay. An even more famous legend is the emperor's rendezvous with the legendary goddess Xiwangmu, or Uma, who met only two Chinese rulers, Emperor Wu of Han and Mu of Zhou (almost 3,000 years earlier).

---

[6]Chung, Tan, *China: A 5,000 Year Odyssey*, New Delhi: SAGE Publications, 2018, p. 1422.

Han Dynasty's China could not win any campaign against the Xiongnu until the reign of Emperor Wu. To ensure China's long-term security, Emperor Wu abandoned the appeasement policy and became determined to free China from the Xiongnu tribe once and for all. He allied with several Central Asian states to jointly fight the Xiongnu, weakening them after a dozen fierce battles. Later, Han Emperor Yuan, who reigned from 49 to 33 BCE, also united with the Central Asian countries to drive out the Xiongnu. It took China over a century to protect itself from this serious threat and secure its northern territory. Although people thought that the Xiongnu had finally vanished, this was not the case. The Huns, originating from the Caspian Sea, entered the Caucasus around 150 CE and became a large kingdom within the domain of the Roman Empire from the fourth century onwards.

The expansion of the Han forces in Central Asia after the collapse of this Xiongnu confederacy contributed to the Chinese awareness of the southern Hindu Kush in the present-day Afghanistan-Pakistan region. Such information was gathered from various travellers, and most likely, also from the military and espionage activities of the Han court in the region. The Han court tried several times to install a friendly regime in its Central Asian frontier region and to exact tribute from polities located in the area.

When Emperor Wu exerted all of China's energy into fighting the Xiongnu, he sent out several Han envoys on diplomatic missions and international trade. Zhang Qian was the most famous envoy (164–114 BCE). After returning from his first sojourn in Central Asia, he told Emperor Wu of his discovery of Shu cloth—silk fabrics from Sichuan—which he had seen in Daxia (now Afghanistan). He had been told that Indian traders were re-exporting these fabrics. Upon enquiry about the route through which the products reached the local market, Zhang was told that they came via a polity in the south called Shendu. This is the first mention of the name in Chinese records, which became associated with India in the following centuries. Zhang Qian is also credited for inaugurating the Silk Road, which linked the markets of Han China to those in Rome. Emperor Wu showed great interest in the report and sent emissaries to Central Asia and from Sichuan to Yunnan to contact the Indians directly. However, both efforts failed.

Behind the story of the Silk Road, therefore, is the rise and fall of nomadic confederations and sedentary societies, the consolidation and dissolution of kingdoms and empires, the exchange of commodities and fine crafts, and the transfer and amalgamation of ideas, religions, technology, science, art, architecture, myths and legends. These lay claim to the artefacts, heritage sites and symbolic meaning of the Silk Road for political and economic purposes and to build their national identity. For these reasons, the Silk Road can not only be seen as a demarcated route with a linear history, but also as a series of attitudes and relationships with the past, involving particular people at particular points in history for particular reasons. One wonders about certain parts of the Silk Road's past that lie buried in the sands of the Taklamakan, in dusty museum warehouses or long-forgotten archives.

Tan Chung traces the history of the Silk Road even further back to the Sanxingdui Civilization, which, according to him, was the time when China became known as the country of silk. Chung traces the resonances between the ancient Sanxingdui Civilization, which existed 3,000–6,000 years ago (2800–1000 BCE)—the time of the ancient Shu kingdom, of which there are few references in Chinese records—and the contemporary Indian civilization through the archaeological evidence found in the modern areas of Sichuan and Guanghan, where this civilization flourished.[7] Sichuan is the home of silk, and according to Tan Chung, the Sanxingdui Civilization contributed significantly to the export of raw silk, silk fabrics, and even silkworms, which was supposedly a

---

[7]Ibid., pp. 536–548.

great trade secret. His conclusion is based on Chanakya's mention of China and cloth in *Arthashastra*, a treatise on statecraft he had authored. Chanakya lived in the late fourth century BCE, so it is unclear whether he was referring to an earlier time or his own. Still, one is inclined to believe that he saw or knew about the Chinese silk cocoon. Tan Chung refers to Chang'an (now Xian) as the starting point of the Silk Road.

Chang'an and Pataliputra were two of the greatest cities during the second century BCE. However, they were not the size of today's big metropolitan cities—their populations being less than a million. Chang'an was also centuries away from being a thriving international trade city, as it later became during the Sui and Tang dynasties. At the same time, King Ashoka (304–232 BCE) vigorously spread Buddhism all over the world during his reign. This movement created an international highway, the Dharmaratna-Marg, or the Road of the Buddha-Dharma Jewel. The Dharmaratna-Marg began in Pataliputra and reached Chang'an through Afghanistan, the Central Asian states and western China. Most eminent Buddhist monks from India and other countries reached China via this road.

This road also facilitated the transport of jewels, perfumes, incense, spices and high-quality cotton fabrics from India to China. According to Tan Chung, this road was later known as the Silk Road. The names Dharmaratna-Marg and Silk Road were used interchangeably. Today's Xian, the erstwhile Chang'an, was the starting point of the Silk Road and the destination of the Dharmaratna-Marg—a two-way highway. According to Tan Chung, this route is so dearly remembered by the Chinese Civilization that it has been magnificently depicted in numerous Chinese paintings. Overall, the road fared well for 200 years until the emergence of Wang Mang (45 BCE–23 CE), who became an imperial officer in 22 BCE with backing from his paternal aunt, Empress Dowager Wang, who was the de facto supreme authority. He became a high-ranking officer at the age of 24, and his popularity in government circles soared as he was diligent, capable, flexible and skilled in political games.

Changing Scenario at the Onset of the Common Era

In the first century of the Common Era, the reigning Han Emperor Ping (reigned 1 BCE–6 CE) died while Wang Mang's aunt, Empress Wang, still wielded power. Wang Mang became the de facto ruler and installed a pseudo-emperor, a two-year-old baby, on the throne. After quelling a revolt, he proclaimed himself emperor in 7 CE and changed the dynasty's name from Han to Xin (meaning new). In 23 CE, a rebellious peasant group called Green Forest Army stormed the capital of Chang'an and killed Wang Mang, ending the Xin Dynasty.

That there were already close connections between India and China is clear from an episode narrated by Tan Chung, which, according to him, has not drawn the international attention it should have. An account in the annals of the Han Dynasty mentions that a foreign country on the Indian coast called Huangzhi had an unusual relationship with Wang Mang's regime. At Wang Mang's request, the ruler of Huangzhi sent a rhinoceros as a gift to boost Wang Mang's reputation.

The famous Chinese scientist and statesman Zhang Heng (78–139 CE) wrote in his composition on Chang'an that there were rare animals in the Imperial Park—one with 'huge ears and a folding nose' (depicting an elephant) and another with a 'pointed forehead and short neck' (depicting a rhinoceros). 'China did not have any rhinoceroses, so this one must have been a gift from Huangzhi to Wang Mang.'[8] It must have been hard to transport a rhinoceros from India to China then, but the daunting maritime journey must have been undertaken because of a strong bilateral relationship. Unfortunately, no details about the China-Huangzhi

---

[8]Ibid., p. 1520.

relationship are known. The identity of Huangzhi is also not clear. A conventional theory posits Huangzhi as the Chinese approximation of the Indian word 'Kanchipuram'. From the historical backdrop of the Chinese–Indian contacts, Huangzhi should be Bengal, known for elephants' teeth and rhinoceroses' horns.

Wang Mang's death and the end of the Xin Dynasty gave Liu Xiu, born Guangwu (5 BCE–57 CE), the opportunity to demonstrate his statesmanship. He restored the Han Dynasty and extended its reign for another two centuries. He spent four years quelling rebellions before reunifying Tianxia and moving the capital to Luoyang, making a fresh start. The new phase of the Han Dynasty was called Eastern Han because Luoyang, the new capital, was to the east of Chang'an, the old capital.

Golden Deity and Arrival of Buddhists in China

Liu Zhuang (28–75 CE), son and successor of Emperor Guangwu, who reigned as Han Emperor Ming for 18 years (57–75 CE), was considered a mediocre ruler compared to his father. However, it was he who initiated the warm millennial welcome to the advent of Indian civilization in China. This began with the story, well-known in Chinese tradition, of Emperor Ming's dream featuring the Golden Deity. In 65 CE, Emperor Ming was said to have dreamt of a giant golden deity, 16 feet tall, with a brilliant halo around his neck, flying inside the palace. The following day, the grand historian at his court, Fu Yi, told him that there was such a deity called Buddha in the West. Emperor Ming immediately sent a party led by Cai Yin to the western regions (Central Asia and India) in search of the deity. The party returned to Luoyang (around 64–75 CE) with two eminent Indian monks, namely Kashyapa Matanga and Dharmaratna or Dharmaraksha (also known as Gobharana or Zhu Falan).[9]

---

[9]Ibid., p. 1546.

Born to a Kashyapa family and named Matanga, Kashyapa
Matanga was a shaman of Magadha. But when the Chinese envoy
came to India, he was living in Gandhara. Matanga received
the envoy there, who gave him the imperial offer. He agreed to
undertake the arduous journey to China, travelling over steep hills
and deserts. Accompanying Matanga was Dharmaratna, who also
came from Central India and was a very learned man who had
been a guru to several savants in India. According to some accounts,
when he received the invitation from the Chinese emperor, his king
did not allow him to leave. He was, however, very excited about
the invitation and succeeded in stealing away from his province.

Emperor Ming was thrilled to receive these learned guests
and built the now-famous Monastery of White Horses—named
as such because the two Indian monks had arrived on white
horses—to accommodate them so that they could translate
Buddhist scriptures to make Chinese assets out of the integral
elements of the Indian civilization. This episode highlights the
warm welcome of the Indian civilization by the Chinese. The
emperor ensured that the stay of the two monks was comfortable
in the newly built monastery and then asked them to translate
the Buddhist scriptures. Emperor Ming Ti's partiality towards the
Indian monks roused the jealousy of others. The Taoists tried to
work against them, as did the Confucians. This struggle continued
for several years before Buddhism could secure its pride of place.
Emperor Ming Ti wanted to know the superiority of either religion
and ordered that a test be done under his supervision. Buddhism
emerged victorious, forcing the emperor to accept the Buddha's
Dhamma from the Indian monks.

While staying at the White Horse Monastery, the two
monks studied the Chinese language with great zeal. Many new
converts flocked to Kashyapa Matanga to learn the teachings
of the Buddha. Still, he did not like to talk about them as he
could only communicate in the language of the Chinese frontier
that the monks had picked up on their way to China. As the

Chinese Buddhists kept pressing him to impart the teachings of the Buddha, he brought out a Chinese version of the sacred book with the help of his colleague Dharmaraksha, in the form of the *sutra* (short aphoristic texts) of 42 sections spoken by the Buddha. Thus, the two monks completed a book in Chinese titled *Canon* (which unfortunately does not exist today), which contained 42 chapters, marking the beginning of Buddhism in China. It is said that Kashyapa Matanga concealed his excellent understanding and did not translate many works but simply chose this sutra to teach others about the great ideas of Buddha. He continued to stay at the White Horse Monastery until the end of his days. After his death, his work was carried on by Dharmaraksha, who translated at least five Sanskrit works between 68 and 70 CE.

As early as the first century CE, Buddhists from India and Central Asia arrived in China and chose to live and preach atop hillsides and remote locations, erecting temples and building societies. They built villages and townships to disseminate Buddhist Dhamma. Pilgrims visited these places, and poets arrived to carve their art on rocks or leave it in Buddhist temples. There are some amusing stories about how Buddhism spread. For example, the arrival of the Indian monk whose original name may have been Matiyukta—although he is better known by the Chinese name Hui Li—was a remarkable phenomenon of 'charm creation' in China. Although there is no reference to him in Indian history, this story is often told in Chinese literature.

According to Chinese records, Hui Li sailed from the West, the 'heavenly' India, and arrived in China in the 320s. He is said to have settled in Hangzhou in Zhejiang province, a remote place with sparsely scattered villages. He used to meditate atop a rock on a hill by the West Lake, which has now become one of the most popular tourist attractions in the world. Gradually, he gained a small following and told the local people that the hill had been a familiar spot in India, Lingjuishan, Chinese variant of the Sanskrit Gridhrakuta (hill of the sacred kite, commonly known as Vulture Peak). Indian readers may be familiar with this name as it is said to have been the Buddha's favourite retreat in Rajagriha in modern-day Bihar. The story goes that Reverend Hui Li told the local people, who were mostly his followers, that the hill he was meditating on was part of the Magadha Kingdom, known in China as the 'heavenly' Central India, and that it had flown to Hangzhou by the divine power of the Buddha. The locals were mystified but sceptical. Seeing their reaction, Hui Li declared that he could prove his claim as he knew the hill quite well and his old friends who lived there could attest to his claim. He then uttered some strange cries and down came a troop of monkeys out of the jungle right in their midst. The locals were convinced, and the news that a hill had flown there from India spread far and wide.

The First Three Centuries of the Common Era

Other monks followed in Kashyapa Matanga's footsteps, and Buddhism began to gain ground in China. Although Indian Buddhist monks led the development of Chinese Buddhist literature, their translations were not perfect as the monks couldn't master the Chinese language in such a short period. Their only purpose in translation was to somehow make the teachings of the Buddha available to the Chinese. Only at the time of Xuanzang did a proper translation of the literature begin.

After Ming Ti died in 76 CE, his successor invited several other Indian scholar-monks. The Tibetan authorities mention Aryakala, Sthavirachilu, Kaksha and Shramana Suvinya in the first century and Dharmakala in the second. In some cases, only the Chinese names of these Indians are known. Six prominent Indian monks are mentioned in the early stages of the introduction of Buddhism in China: Tchu Fa-soh, Mahabala, Dharmakala, Vighna, Tchou Luh-yen and Dharmapala.

Tchou Fa-soh came at the end of the second century. He, too, lived in the White Horse Monastery in Luoyang and translated two sutras between 172 and 183 CE. Mahabala also lived in the monastery and translated some texts around the same time. In the third century, Dharmapala took a text from Kapilavastu, which he translated with the help of Khau Man-Sian, a shaman of Tibetan origin who came to China from Central India.

Gradually, these Indian monks tried to build up Chinese Buddhism. Whenever any error was discovered in the deportment, behaviour, or way of life of the monks, or the collective, the organizers tried to set it right. However, when Dharmakala went from Central India to China in 222 CE, he found the Chinese were quite ignorant of the rules of *Vinaya*, which were essential in the lives of Buddhist monks, as the Buddha himself had been very particular about discipline in his sangha. Hence, Dharmakala translated the 'Pratimoksha', a list of rules governing the behaviour of Buddhist monks. It was the first book of the *Vinaya Pitaka* published in Chinese. The *Vinaya Pitaka* is the first division of the *Tripitaka*—the canonical collection of Theravada Buddhist scriptures. It regulates the monastic life and the daily conduct of monks, nuns and the sangha.

Two other Indian monks, Vighna and Luh-yen, went to China in 224 CE. They worked together to translate the *Dhammapada* sutra, a collection of verses that are the teachings of Gautama Buddha, to his disciples. However, as they did not have mastery over the Chinese language, their translation was unsuccessful. Sometimes, Tibetan monks like Khau Man-Sian, who had settled in India, went to China. One of them was Khan-ku, the son of the prime minister of Kamboja. His family had long been settled in India, from where he travelled to Nanjing, the capital of the Wu Dynasty. He became a favourite of Emperor Ming, who erected a new monastery for him. Over time, the number of monasteries began to increase. Khan-ku was a great worker and is said to have translated 14 works of Buddhism.

The Turning Point in Chinese Buddhist Literature

A significant moment in the history of Buddhist literature in China came when it was dominated by a man named Kumarjiva. He had an Indian father and his family exercised the rights of hereditary ministers in an Indian state. However, his father renounced his claim to the ministership and became a Buddhist monk. When he went to the ancient Buddhist kingdom of Kucha, its king requested that he become his *rajguru*. While he was staying in Kucha as a royal preceptor, the king's sister fell in love with him and eventually married him. Around 344 CE, they had a son named Kumarjiva, a combination of their names 'Kumara' and 'Jiva'.

When Kumarjiva was seven years old, his mother took him to a convent called Tsiao-li, where he learnt all the sacred sutras. At the age of nine, he went to Kashmir, where he studied under the celebrated Acharya Bandhudatta. After three years, his mother returned with him to Kucha when she met an arhat, who predicted a great future for Kumarjiva. In Kachgar, Kumarjiva studied the *Abhidharma* with six *pada*s (sections). The king of Kashgar was eager to retain Kumarjiva in his court, but the king of Kucha sent multiple consecutive messengers, asking him to return. So, Kumarjiva returned to Kucha and was personally welcomed by the king.

He was ordained at the age of 20 and began to live in a new monastery built by the king. Meanwhile, driven by his spirit of adventure, Vimalaksha, a celebrated shramana of Kashmir, travelled to the far-off kingdom of Kucha, where he met Kumarjiva and taught him the *Vinaya* texts. While Kumarjiva was in Kucha, Lu Koang, a general of the former Tsin Dynasty of China, attacked the kingdom and defeated its king. Kumarjiva was among the prisoners taken by Lu Koang. In 401 CE, Kumarjiva's life reached a turning point when he went to the imperial court of the Second Tsin Dynasty at Chang'an. The Chinese king Yao Hhin cordially welcomed him.

At Emperor Yao's request, Kumarjiva began translating Sanskrit Buddhist texts into Chinese and completed more than a hundred translations within 12 years with the help of his Indian friends and Chinese disciples. He commanded the respect of more than 1,000 disciples. Some of them became famous for their own writings, the most notable of whom was Fa-hien.

Although neither language was his mother tongue, he had an extraordinary command over both. He developed his literary style, making his translations feel like original works. No *tantras* (Buddhist mystical texts) or *dharanis* (mantras in Mahayana Buddhism) were found among his works, as he was supposedly enthusiastic about neither. Instead, his imagination was occupied with books on meditation and *samadhi*, and the *Pragyaparamitas*—principal texts of Mahayana Buddhism. He also wrote the biographies of Ashvaghosha and Nagarjuna.

The Luminaries of the Fourth and Fifth Centuries

Kumarjiva inspired many others to carry on the work he had begun. He successfully trained Chinese monks headed by Fa-hien to propagate Buddhism among his countrymen. Many prominent monks of that time were great writers who produced books on Chinese Buddhist literature within a short period.

Dharmaraksha, Kashyapa Matanga's companion, went to China around 381 CE. He was a literary genius credited with an extraordinary output of Chinese translations (at least 61, if not more). He mastered the language within a very short time after he arrived in China and translated a spate of books. He was followed almost immediately by Gautama Sangha Deva, a shramana from Kashmir, who translated at least seven books. Buddhabhadra followed suit in 398 CE. He claimed descent from the Shakya family and was associated with the great Kumarjiva. It was immediately after his arrival that Kumarjiva arrived in China. When Kumarjiva began his literary career, he consulted

Buddhabhadra, amongst others, who cleared many of his doubts. Buddhabhadra also assisted Fa-hien. He worked in China for over 31 years and died there at the age of 71 in 429 CE, having translated at least 15 texts.

Shortly before Buddhabhadra, Sanghabhata left Kabul for China. Not much is known about him, except that he translated three books. In 382 CE, the Indian shaman Dharmapriya arrived in China and translated several texts. It is worth noting that for four centuries, Buddhism in China had only developed through the translation of Buddhist Sanskrit books from India. As a result, Chinese scholars gradually but enthusiastically began to learn Sanskrit. Fa-hien took a fundamental step in this direction by journeying to India and returning to China with authentic Buddhist texts.

While Kumarjiva was making a name for himself in China, his guru, Vimalaksha, happened to come to the same kingdom and met his old pupil in 406 CE. Unfortunately, Kumarjiva died in 413 CE. After his death, Vimalaksha went southwards and translated two works. He died in 418 CE at the age of 77.

In 414 CE, a scholar-monk named Dharmaksema was active in China. He arrived at the same time as the scholars from Kashmir, although he hailed from Central India. He was invited by Emperor Tsu-khu-man-sun (reigned 403–433 CE) of the Northern Lian Dynasty.[10] Dharmaksema began translating vigorously and completed seven texts in seven years. His fame as a Buddhist scholar spread far and wide. Taiwu, an emperor of the Wei Dynasty (42–452 CE), invited him to his capital. This gravely offended his former patron, who wanted to keep Dharmaksema in his kingdom. This rivalry between the two sovereigns ultimately became the cause of his death. When Dharmaksema honoured the request of his new patron, his old patron got angry and had him murdered while he was on his way to meet his new patron.

---

[10]Bose, Phanindra Nath, *The Indian Teachers in China*, S. Ganesan Publisher, Tamil Nadu, 1923, p. 72.

Fa-hien

The early translators did not try to provide detailed information about the sites and places mentioned in the Buddhist texts. This trend changed in the fifth century when the Chinese monk Fa-hien travelled to South Asia and returned to write his travelogue *Foguoji* (*A Record of the Buddhistic Kingdoms*). Fa-hien embarked on his journey to South Asia in 399 CE. By this time, the route connecting the urban centres of China with the Buddhist sites in South Asia was well-known and frequently traversed by traders and Buddhist missionaries from various parts of Asia. There may have been other Chinese monks before Fa-hien who attempted to visit the Buddhist holy land, India, but it is unclear if anyone before him completed the journey.

Fa-hien's *Foguoji* was the first detailed Chinese account of the sacred Buddhist sites in South Asia. It also described the overland and maritime routes that connected China with South Asia's urban centres and ports. More importantly, it inspired other Chinese Buddhists to make similar trips to India. At the same time, Fa-hien's work triggered a broader discussion among Chinese intellectuals about Indic culture and society vis-à-vis the Sinitic Civilization. This dialogue continued into the twentieth century.

As he explained in his travelogue, Fa-hien's purpose for visiting South Asia was to bring back the monastic rules followed in the region, only a few of which had been rendered into Chinese before he undertook the journey. For Fa-hien, South Asia was more than a mere repository of religious texts; it was also a sacred site with the relics and traces of the Buddha and the commemorative monuments built by King Ashoka, the leading supporter of the doctrine. As a result, the geographical space he witnessed, experienced and wrote about was viewed through the prism of a pilgrim visiting his holy land. The descriptions of South Asia also formed the framework for his views found in the translated Buddhist stories and teachings he had read before embarking on his journey. However, Fa-hien added many details about the region that were not available in the Buddhist texts: the distances between the various towns of South Asia, the mountains and rivers that lay in between, the layout and architecture of the cities, the beliefs and customs of the people, and the practice of Buddhism in the monastic institutions. Fa-hien's records vividly describe the Pamir Mountains, the Himalayan ranges, the great rivers of Indus, Yamuna and Ganga, cities such as Pataliputra and Varanasi, and the port of Tamralipta (Tamralipti). He also recorded his voyages by ship, first from Tamralipta to Sinhala and then across the Bay of Bengal through Southeast Asia to China.

For the readers of Fa-hien's travelogue in China, his descriptions confirmed the existence of the sites mentioned in the translated text, corroborated the utopic nature of these places, and provided detailed information about the distant foreign land that had already entered the Chinese imagination. The fact that Fa-hien's record was widely read in China is evident from the citations of his work across Buddhist and non-Buddhist texts. Perhaps the most significant statement based on Fa-hien's description appeared in the work *Shui Jing Zhu* by Li Daoyoan, a geographer of the sixth century CE.

Li referred to the region from Mathura to the south as Madhyadesha—its people were rich and dressed and ate like the people of the Middle Kingdom of China. Fa-hien's account may have contributed not only to expanding knowledge of the geography of South Asia but also to an elevation of the Chinese perception of South Asian society and culture. Perhaps because of such eyewitness accounts by Chinese Buddhist monks, the court scribes in China became less ethnocentric in their description of South Asians than other foreign regions and their peoples.

In the period between the fifth century, when Fa-hien composed his work, and the mid-seventh century, when Xuanzang—the other renowned Chinese traveller to South Asia—

gave a more detailed account of the Buddhist holy land, new knowledge-circulation networks emerged. The most important of these were the diplomatic channels. In the period between Fahien and Xuanzang, several diplomatic missions from South Asia arrived in the courts of the Chinese rulers. In the Chinese dynastic histories from this period, two letters brought by representatives from the region that the Chinese called Middle India have been preserved. The first is found in the *Song Shu*, which covers the history of the Liu Song Dynasty that ruled China from 420 to 479 CE. Written by a ruler named Yueai (perhaps Chandragupta II) from a polity called Jiabili, the letter was delivered to Emperor Wen in the fifth year of the Yuanjia reign.

Buddhist Monks from Kashmir

Several Buddhist scholars travelled from Kashmir to China around this time. Buddhayasas translated multiple texts at the beginning of the fifth century. He was followed by Dharmayasas (who translated two to three texts in eight years), a student of Punyatrata (who went to China around 400 CE), one of Kumarjiva's colleagues from Kashmir. Buddhajiva from Kashmir went to China in 428 CE. Only three works are credited to him. One of the last monks of the Kashmiri group was Dharmamitra, who reached China in 424 CE and continued the work of translation until 441 CE, soon after which he died. Among the greatest travellers from Kashmir was Gunavarman. By the time he arrived in China, he had already converted the island of Java to Buddhism. Gunavarman descended from the royal family of Kashmir. Although his ancestors had governed the kingdom for a long time, at the time of his birth, his father, Sanghananda, was living in the forest as an exile because his grandfather Haribhadra had been banished from his kingdom for his harshness.

When Gunavarman was 18 years old, it was prophesied that he would govern the kingdom at the age of 30. Gunavarman retired from the world at the age of 20 and became a shaman. At this young age, he had mastered all the Buddhist scriptures and was acknowledged as a master by his contemporaries. When Gunavarman was 30 years old, the king of Kashmir died without leaving an heir. His ministers decided to put Gunavarman on the throne, as he was a member of the royal family. However, when approached, he declined the offer. Soon after, Gunavarman went to Sinhala. After developing the Dharma there, he went to Java. A little earlier, when Fa-hien had visited Java, Hinduism was still flourishing there. It was Gunavarman who converted the people of Java to Buddhism.

Just a day before his arrival, the mother of the king of Java is said to have dreamt that a monk in a swift boat had entered the kingdom. The king of Java persuaded his mother to welcome Gunavarman and accept the Buddha's teachings from him. The king also desired that all people in his kingdom obey and respect the monk; there were to be no killings and gifts were to be given to the poor. After this, the entire kingdom adopted Buddhism.

With this event, Gunavarman's fame spread, attracting the attention of the Chinese shramanas. In 424 CE, they approached Emperor Wen and suggested sending someone to Gunavarman to invite him to the Song territory. The emperor sent the prefect of Kiao Tcheou to take the necessary measures. Some Chinese shramanas were also to accompany him. By a strange coincidence, Gunavarman, who had already left Java on a merchant boat to go to another small kingdom, found that a favourable wind landed him in Canton, which was in the Song territory. When the news reached Emperor Wen, he asked the prefect and the Chinese shramanas to supply all necessary provisions to the Indian monk and send him to the capital.

Gunavarman spent a year in Che-Hing on his way to the capital. He found that the mountain Hou-che resembled the Gridhrakuta Mountain, one of Buddha's most famous abodes; accordingly, the mountain's name was changed to the Peak of Vulture. The prefect of

Che-Hing immensely admired Gunavarman. When he was about to die, the Indian monk went to see him and preach the Dharma. In the meantime, Emperor Wen became anxious to see Gunavarman and requested that he come to the capital quickly. He arrived in Nanking in 431 CE, where the emperor received him personally and requested to be instructed in the Dharma as he did not wish to kill but was obliged to do so because of the exigencies of the time. The emperor then arranged for Gunavarman to stay at the Jetavana Vihara monastery and equipped it with all the required facilities.

Gunavarman began his work. Another monk, Ishvara, had undertaken the translation of one of the texts but was unable to continue and had left it incomplete. Gunavarman completed this translation. One of his great works was to organize a sangha of Chinese nuns. Until then, Chinese women had not turned to Buddhism in a significant way. There were only a few Sinhalese nuns who had been in China for six years, but no rules were framed. Now, the nuns sought to organize themselves into a sangha and approached Gunavarman to frame the rules. He was willing to do this, but they did not have the requisite number of nuns required to form a sangha. Since there were no other nuns in the Song territory, Gunavarman asked them to reach the desired number by inviting new nuns from foreign countries, who were then ordained. Gunavarman breathed his last in China at the age of 67. He was not a great translator like Kumarjiva—he translated only ten works—but he did much to spread Buddhism and improve the spiritual welfare of people.

The Arrival of Further Monks into China from India

At the end of the fifth century, several more Indian monks went to China. Among them were Gunabhadra and Tchou Fa-kieu (known only by his Chinese name). Gunabhadra arrived from Central India four years after Gunavarman. He was from a Brahmin family and was so well-versed in all branches of the Mahayana School that he was given the nickname Mahayana. Coming to China in 435 CE, he vigorously began his translation work and continued with it for the next eight years, translating at least 78 texts. He is therefore considered one of the greatest translators of the period. He died at the age of 75 in 468 CE. Tchou Fa-kieu translated six works between 465 and 471 CE. In 481 CE, Dharmajalayasas left Central India for China. Somehow, only one work of translation is ascribed to him. Gunavridhi was the last monk to arrive in China at the end of the fifth century. He also belonged to Central India and translated three works between 492 and 495 CE.

Advents in the Sixth Century

Indian monks flocked to China in the sixth century. At its onset, the prominent ones were Dharmaruci, Ratnamati, Gautam Pragyaruci, Upasunaya and Vimoksha Pragyaruci. Dharmaruci was from the southern part of India. He translated three works between 504 and 507 CE. He was followed by Ratnamati from Central India, who translated three texts, including the *Mahayanottara-Tantra Shastra*.[11] This indicates that Tantra (the Vajrayana sect of Buddhism) made an incursion into China around this time. The introduction of Tantrism was responsible for producing numerous dharanis and tantras in China.

The great translator Bodhiruci, who hailed from North India, arrived around the same time. He stopped at Luoyang in 508 CE and obtained command over the Chinese language in a very short time. Although he was not as prolific as Kumarjiva and Amoghvajra (who arrived much later), he provided outstanding service to Buddhism through his translations. In 27 years, he produced over 30 of them. Budhasanta went to China in 524 CE and stayed for about 25 years, translating about ten texts. Gautam

---

[11]Ibid., p. 85.

Pragyaruci went from Varanasi, and in three years—from 538 to 541 CE—he translated about 18 works. Upasunaya, like many of his predecessors, was the son of a king—he was the heir to the throne of Udyana. However, he gave up the crown and became a monk. He found his way to China and translated three works in the capital of the Eastern Wei Dynasty between 538 and 540 CE. Later, he went southward and translated one more work in Nanking in 545 CE. He also received a Sanskrit text from a Khotanese monk in 558 CE and translated it in 565 CE.

Vimoksha Pragyaruci also arrived from Udyana. He claimed descent from the Shakya family of Kapilavastu and worked in collaboration with another Indian monk, Gautam Pragyaruci, to translate five works. The sixth century witnessed the advent of great writers such as Narendrayasas, Jinagupta and his *acharyas*. They served Buddhism despite being mistreated by the non-Buddhist emperors of China. They fled and lived in exile as long as non-Buddhist emperors ruled China. After the revival of Buddhism, they returned to take up the translation work.

Narendrayasas was the predecessor of Jinagupta. He finally landed in Ye, the capital of the Chi Dynasty, in 556 CE. After arriving in China, he began living at T'ien Ping Monastery, where he started translating Buddhist texts and completed the translation of seven works. All sections of people loved him for his deep learning and admirable virtues and held him in high esteem for his holiness. However, a sudden change came about in China's politics. The Tsin Dynasty, under whose patronage Narendrayasas lived and worked, was destroyed by the T-cheau Dynasty in 577 CE. With this, the whole imperial policy changed. Buddhism lost its place, and Emperor Wu banished it altogether from the region. Narendrayasas, along with other monks, had to go into exile. However, the T-cheau Dynasty was soon replaced by the Souei Dynasty in 581 CE, which again established authority at Chang'an.

The rise of the Souei Dynasty led to the revival of Buddhism. The Chinese mission, which had visited India between 575 and 581 CE, had been stopped in the territory of the Turks because of the exile of Buddhism from China and finally proceeded to its native land. The emperor of the new dynasty welcomed the monks. They had brought many Sanskrit texts from India with them and a competent Indian monk was needed to translate them. Immediately, the choice fell on Narendrayasas, who was invited to the capital after his exile in 582. Narendrayasas lived in the Ta-hing-chan Monastery, where he undertook translations of the newly brought books at the emperor's request. This was the first time the emperor appointed a translation board, presided over by Narendrayasas. Thirty shramanas were found and placed at his disposal to assist him with the work. With their help, he translated eight works between 582 and 585 CE.

However, the translations were not up to the mark since they contained some inaccuracies. A more learned Indian monk was required and the choice fell on Jinagupta, who was also living in exile with the Turks. Narendrayasas undertook no new work until the arrival of Jinagupta. They lived in the Kouan Monastery. Narendrayasas lived for another four years and died in China in 589 CE. Another Indian monk, Paramartha, had come to China before Narendrayasas. He hailed from Ujjain and arrived in Nanking in 548 CE. He lived in China for 21 years, from 548 to 569 CE. He translated around fifty works before his death at the age of 71 in 569 CE.

Jinagupta arrived in China in 557 CE with his two acharyas, Jnanabhadra and Jnanayasas, and another disciple, Yasogupta. Jnanabhadra, the guru of Yasogupta and Jinagupta, only produced one work with the help of the other three monks. Jnanayasas, on the other hand, translated six works with the help of his two disciples, Yasogupta and Jinagupta. Yasogupta translated three or four works together with Jnanayasas and Jinagupta.

Jinagupta was a shramana of the kingdom of Gandharva and an inhabitant of Purushapura (present-day Peshawar), which became the capital of the Kushan kingdom. His family name was

Kambhu and he claimed to be a Kshatriya. He was the youngest son of his parents and had had a religious bent of mind since childhood. At the tender age of seven, he wanted to renounce the world. He faced no opposition from his parents and retired to the Mahayana Vihara. He was fortunate to have Jnanayasas and Jnanabhadra as his teachers as they instructed him in various fields of learning, and it was due to them that he became such a great scholar.

Jinagupta was one of the most productive writers who worked in China. Emperor Kao-Tsou of the Souei Dynasty requested Jinagupta to translate some Indian astronomical texts apart from the Buddhist ones, with the assistance of several other Indian and Chinese monks. Jinagupta died in 600 CE at the age of 78. His contributions were no less than those of Kumarjiva and Bodhiruci. Towards the close of the sixth century, three more monks arrived in China. They were Dharmagyana, Vinita Ruci and Dharmagupta. Gautam Dharmagyana hailed from Varanasi and was the eldest son of Gautam Pragyaruci, who had visited China in 538 CE. While in China, he was entrusted with some administrative work. After the destruction of the Northern Tshi Dynasty in 577 CE, he was appointed governor of the Yan-sen district by the Northern Kau Dynasty. In 582 CE, Wan-ti, the first emperor of the Tsui Dynasty, called him to his capital, where he translated a text. Vinita Ruci was a shaman from Udyana who reached China in 582 CE. He translated only two texts. The last shaman of the sixth century, Dharmagupta, followed the same route as Jinagupta and arrived in Chang'an in 590 CE. He translated more than ten texts between 590 and 619 CE, the year of his death.

The Seventh-Century Slowdown

The seventh century did not see the arrival of many Indian monks for reasons difficult to fathom—only six monks left India for China. The first shaman of this century was Prabhakaramitra, descended from a Kshatriya family of Central India. He went to China in 627 CE during the Than Dynasty. He translated only three texts and died at 69 in 633 CE.

In 652 CE, O-ti-khu-to went to China. He hailed from Central India, and in two years, could only produce one work. He was followed by Nadi, who reached China in 655 CE. Before coming to China, he had travelled all over India and Sinhala and collected 1,500 texts of the *Tripitaka*s, the Buddhist scriptures, and the Hinayana and Mahayana schools. In 656 CE, the Chinese emperor sent him to secure some medicine from a distant island, from where he returned in 663 CE and translated three works. Divakara was another monk who travelled to China from Central India. In 12 years, 676–688 CE, he translated 18 works. After him came Ratnacinta from Kashmir. Between 698 and 706 CE, he translated seven works. He lived a long life and died in China at the age of 100 in 721 CE. The end of the seventh century saw a great Indian monk in China, Dharmaruci, who worked on the translations for about twenty years from 693 to 713 CE. He belonged to the Kashyapa clan of a Brahmin family of South India. When he went to China, Empress Wu (684–705 CE) changed his name to Bodhiruci. He translated no less than 53 books. The details of his life are unknown, but it is said that he died in 727 CE at the age of 156.

Eighth Century

In the eighth century, the first Indian monk was Pramiti, a shramana of Central India. He translated only one work with the assistance of another Indian shramana, Meghashikha from Udyana, and a Chinese monk. He was followed by Vajrabodhi, who was from a Brahmin family in South India. He arrived in China in 719 CE and translated four works between 723 CE and 730 CE. He died at the age of 71 in 732 CE. The next scholar was from the University of Nalanda, Subhakara Simha. He went to

China in 716 CE with a few Sanskrit texts. He translated four of them by 730 CE and died in China in 735 CE.

The foremost Buddhist scholar, monk and translator who visited China in this century was Amoghvajra. He had the calibre of his renowned predecessors, Kumarjiva, Jinagupta and Bodhiruci. Being a Tantric scholar, he also spread Tantrism in China—translating numerous dharanis and tantras. Amoghvajra was a shramana from a North Indian Brahmin family. He accompanied his guru, Vajrabodhi, to China in 719 CE. On his deathbed in 732 CE, Vajrabodhi asked him to return to India to collect new texts. Nine years later, in 741 CE, he left China for India. He travelled throughout India and Sinhala for four years and returned to China in 746 CE. He then commenced his work in China, which attracted royal attention. The reigning emperor Hhuen-Tsun was so pleased with him that he conferred the title of the 'Repository of Wisdom' on him.

In 749 CE, Amoghvajra wanted to return to India. The emperor granted him permission but later went back on his word. Amoghvajra had barely reached the seashore when he received the royal decree calling him back and was thus detained in China. In 756 CE, when he was living in the Hhintse-Shan Monastery and continuing his translation work, new honours were bestowed on him by the emperor. He received the royal edict to translate works to be included in the official Chinese *Tripitaka*. In 771 CE, Amoghvajra presented his translation, which comprised seventy-seven works, as a birthday gift to Emperor Tai-tsun (763–779 CE). After achieving this Herculean feat, he died in 774 CE at the age of 70. More honours were conferred on him posthumously by the emperor.

Ninth Century onwards

In the ninth century, the travels of Indian monks to China had petered out. Nonetheless, in 972 CE, the Indian monks K'o-tche, Fa-k'ien, Tchen-li, and San-ko-t'o went to China.

The great Indian monk Dharmadeva arrived in 973 CE from Nalanda. He was among the most celebrated translators during the Song Dynasty (960–1127 CE). In eight years (973–981 CE), he translated 46 works. In 982 CE, he was honoured by Emperor Theitsun (reigned from 976 to 999 CE). Many dharanis and tantras had become popular among the translated works in China and Tibet. By this time, the University of Nalanda had become a centre of Tantric Buddhism, and Dharmadeva may have received his texts from there. The Indian monks who had developed the Tantric School in Tibet and translated the tantras into Tibetan mainly came from Nalanda and Vikramshila. Dharmadeva died in 1000 CE and was posthumously honoured by the emperor. He was one of the last great monks to come from India to China.

Manjushri, a prince, the son of the king of western India, went to China in 971 CE. He lived in the Siang-kono Monastery. He was a virtuous monk who became popular in the city and received many gifts. Other monks soon became jealous of him and informed the emperor that Manjushri was homesick and wanted permission to return to India. An imperial order permitted him. When Manjushri learnt of this, he was furious but helpless. He ostensibly started for India a few months later, but no one knew where he went.

In 980 CE, two celebrated translators of the Song period, Tiensi-tsai and Tche-hu, arrived in China. The monk Tien-si-tsai is said to have come from Kashmir, but according to some, he hailed from Jalandhara. He was honoured by the emperor in 982 CE, the same year when a board was formed by the imperial order to translate Buddhist texts. It consisted of Dharmadeva, Tien-si-tsai, and Danapala, each of whom was asked to translate one work. Other Chinese monks well-versed in Sanskrit, such as Fa-hien, were asked to supervise the translations. Others, such as Yangyue and Tchang-ki, were asked to perfect the translation. Tien-si-tsai translated 18 texts in 20 years before he passed away in the year 1000 CE and was honoured posthumously.

Another illustrious translator, Chu-hu, who could be the same person as Danapala, arrived with Tien-si-tsai in 980 CE. He, too, was honoured by the emperor in 982 CE and asked to translate Indian sutras together with Dharmadeva. Chu-hu is said to have translated around 111 books. He is also responsible for producing many dharanis that became so popular that they formed a considerable part of Chinese Buddhist literature. During 984–987 CE, To-lo-men, a Buddhist shramana, was in China. In 990 CE, the monk Pou-t'o-k'i-to arrived from the University of Nalanda with some relics and texts. Kia-lo-cheu-ti, which could probably translate to Kalashanti, visited China in 995 CE. He was also a shramana from Central India who brought Buddhist relics and Sanskrit books written on palm leaves for the emperor. Rahul, a shaman from western India, followed him. The last Indian monk of this century, Ni-wei-ni, was a shaman from Central India who, with his companions, carried several texts to China for the emperor.

The Last Phase

The movement of Buddhist missionaries had gone on for a thousand years. Finally, it started coming to an end with the conquest of North India by the Muslims in the early eighth century. However, a few monks continued to brave the journey. In 1004 CE, China was visited by Fa-hu, whose name was probably Dharmaraksha. He hailed from Magadha and carried relics of the Buddha and Sanskrit texts on palm leaves. He was honoured by the emperor in 1054 CE. He translated 12 works and died at the age of 96 CE in 1058 CE. Zih-Khan or Suryayasas, a contemporary of Fa-hu, translated only two works. Another Indian shramana, Tsi-nah-min-toh-lien-toh-lo-mo-min translated only one work.[12] Tshz-likien (whose Indian name was probably Maitreya Buddha)

---

[12]Ibid., 143.

was an Indian monk appointed by the Rajguru of the emperor of the Liao Dynasty (907–1125 CE). He translated five works and was the last Indian monk to visit China.

Indian monks brought a considerable amount of Sanskrit Buddhist literature to China, together with knowledge of Indian astronomy, astrology, music, sculpture and painting. This was a unique movement in the history of the world.

Translated Buddhist texts were one of the primary conduits through which information about the geography of South Asia reached China. The translators of these texts were mostly natives of Central Asia. In almost every such translated work, the polities, towns, and other geographical sites and terrains of South Asia, especially the Gangetic Region, are mentioned. All these sites were associated with the life of the Buddha, his sermons, or the places where he performed miracles. In most cases, they formed part of the opening passage that began with the formulaic stanza, 'Thus I have heard, at one time the Buddha was at X.' The polity of the city of Shravasti and the Jetavana Park or Vihara, for example, are mentioned most frequently in these early texts. Also mentioned are places such as Rajagriha, Varanasi, Magadha, Champa and Kapilavastu. The 16 great urban centres or *mahanagaras*, the Gridhrakuta Mountain, Mount Meru, and the Indic continent of Jambudvipa are also included in these texts. Sometimes, the names of towns and polities in South Asia are transcribed, such as those of Varanasi and Champa, and at other times, they are translated as with Rajagriha.

2

Fa-Hien's Magadha

Fa-hien was the first important Chinese monk to travel to India. By the time he started on his journey, Buddhism was reasonably well-established in China. He said, 'On enquiry, men of those lands agreed in saying, that, according to an ancient tradition, shramanas from India began to carry the sacred books of the Buddha beyond the river [Indus], from the time when the image of Maitreya Bodhisatwa was set up.'[13] The image was set up about 300 years after the Buddha's final passing from the earth, nirvana, or the *Mahaparinirvana*. There is some disagreement as to when the Buddha died. General Cunningham dates it to 477 BCE, forming his opinion partly from an inscription he copied at Gaya in Magadha. Still, dates of the Buddha's death have been proposed to be anytime between 486 and 261 BCE.

Fa-hien, a resident of Chang'an, was grieved to see that the rules of discipline enunciated in the *Vinaya Pitaka*, one of the Buddhist scriptures that elucidate the monastic rules of conduct for

[13]Fa-Hsien, Faxian, *Travels of Fah-hian and Sung-yun, Buddhist Pilgrims From China to India (400 A.D. and 518 A.D.)*, Samuel Beal and Susil Gupta (trans.), Andesite Press, London, 1964, p. 22.

See also: Faxian, *A Record of Buddhistic Kingdoms being an account by the Chinese monk Fa-hien of his travels in India and Ceylon (A.D. 399–414) in Search of the Buddhist Books of Discipline*, James Legge (trans.), Clarendon Press, 1886, p. 27.

monks and nuns, were not being followed in China. The Buddha himself had been quite firm that the laws of the sangha should be meticulously followed, which prompted Fa-hien's journey.

Fa-hien's Quest

Fa-hien's journey was a remarkable feat as the earlier expedition of Zhang Qian, a Chinese general during the reign of the Han Emperor Wu-ti, had failed in 122 BCE. Fa-hien was the first to find a trade route between China and India beyond the control of the Xiongnu. However, Zhang Qian is considered the hero of his failure because he was the first to explore and document the areas of Central Asia.

Centuries after Zhang Qian, Fa-hien succeeded in coming to India, visiting many sacred Buddhist places in Central Asia on his way and later in India and Southeast Asia between 399 and 412 CE. He gave an account of his travels across the land route from China to India, describing the places he visited, the monasteries he saw, and the Buddhist rituals he witnessed and participated in. Although he started his journey with a group of monks, none of them completed it, and Fa-hien was the only one left by the time he returned to China. The account of his travels is remarkable but not too accurate regarding directions and distances. It is full of supernatural descriptions, the belief in the supernatural being strong at this time. For instance, the legend of Gridhrakuta:

> Three le before you reach the top, there is a cavern in the rocks, facing the south, in which Buddha sat in meditation. Thirty paces to the northwest, there is another, where Ananda was sitting in meditation, when the deva Mara Pisuna, having assumed the form of a large vulture, took his place in front of the cavern and frightened the disciple. Then Buddha, by his mysterious, supernatural power, made a

cleft in the rock, introduced his hand, and stroked Ananda's shoulder so that his fear immediately passed away. The footprints of the bird and the cleft for (Buddha's) hand are still there and hence comes the name of 'The Hill of the Vulture Cavern'.[14]

More than two centuries had to elapse before Xuanzang wrote an accurate account of the land route from China to India in the *Great Tang Records on the Western Regions* at the request of Emperor Taizong of the Tang Dynasty. It inspired the novel *Journey to the West*, a classic in Chinese literature written by Wu Cheng'en about nine centuries after Xuanzang's death. Sir Alexander Cunningham later used Xuanzang's records in his excavations of the many sites in India, including Sarnath and Sanchi. He made the first serious attempt to trace the history of Buddhism through its architectural remains. In 1871, he published the *Ancient Geography of India*, the first collection of King Ashoka's edicts.

The Discoveries in Madhyadesha

When Fa-hien came to India, the monasteries were prosperous, although rivalries could already be seen between the Brahminical religion, the Hinayanists and the Mahayanists. They held considerable real estate and assets in Middle India (a term Fa-hein uses to connote the whole of northern India). 'From the time of Buddha's nirvana,' says Fa-hien:

> [...] (T)he kings and nobles of all these countries began to erect Vihâras for the priesthood, and to endow them with lands, gardens, houses, and also men and oxen to cultivate them. The Records of these endowments, being engraved

[14]Faxian, *A Record of Buddhistic Kingdoms being an account by The Chinese Monk Fa-Hien (A.D. 399–414) in Search of the Buddhist Books of Discipline*, James Legge (trans.), Oxford, Clarendon Press, 1886, p. 83.

on sheets of copper, have been handed down from one king
to another, so that no one has dared to deprive them of
possession, and they continue to this day to enjoy their
proper Revenues. All the resident priests have chambers,
beds, coverlets, food, drink and clothes provided for them
without stint or reserve. Thus it is in all places.[15]

The custom of maintaining monasteries with land grants, which
Fa-hien noted in the Madhyadesha, was common throughout
North India. Almost three centuries later, when I-Ching visited
the monasteries of North India, he stated, 'Indian Monasteries
possess special allotment of lands.' Out of the income from the
landed property, supplemented by casual donations, the needs of
resident monks used to be supplied 'without stint'. The prosperity
of the monasteries, together with their tendency to hoard what
was provided to them, prompted I-Ching to strike a somewhat
censuring note: 'It is unseemly for a monastery to have great
wealth, granaries full of rotten corn, many servants, male and
female, money and treasures hoarded in the treasury, without
using any of these things, while all the members are suffering
from poverty.' However, this shows the extent of the prosperity
enjoyed by the monasteries.

Not only kings or members of the aristocracy made these land
grants, but also well-to-do lay Buddhists gave land to sanghas to
earn spiritual merit. It has even suggested that the theory of joint
ownership was developed by the Brahminical logists Yagyavalka
and Vishnu, mainly to prevent a Buddhist member of the joint
family of landed proprietors from alienating the family property
in this way. It may perhaps have become a widespread practice
at the time.

---

[15]Ibid., 43.

Fa-Hsien, Faxian, *Travels of Fah-hian and Sung-yun, Buddhist Pilgrims From
China to India (400 A.D. and 518 A.D.)*, Samuel Beal and Susil Gupta (trans.),
Andesite Press, London, 1964, p. 55.

Although Fa-hien had an eye for the grand and spectacular in the Buddhist rites and ceremonies he witnessed, he did not seem inclined towards architecture and sculpture, for he only described the viharas by saying that he had seen 'great viharas'. However, he did describe in detail some public Buddhist ceremonies that he saw in Madhyadesha—perhaps he was too intent on noting the customary ways of the monks in India to worry about the architecture of the viharas or their sculptural decorations.

The Interim Decline

Over a couple of centuries separate Fa-hien and Xuanzang. When Xuanzang came to India in the seventh century, Buddhism was in a state of decline. In the two intervening centuries, the Huna incursions at the end of the fifth and early sixth centuries weakened the Gupta Empire. The relentless vandalism of Mihirakula—one of the most important rulers of the Alchon Huns of Central Asia— reduced many great viharas in Gandhara, Kashmir and western Uttar Pradesh to ruins during his reign from 502 to 530 CE. Besides, the new Brahminism of the Gupta Age gained influence over Buddhism, reducing the number of viharas and increasing Brahminical establishments. Once famous monasteries were now deserted or in ruins. Fa-Hien had already seen many ruined and deserted monasteries, but they were more prominent in Xuanzang's time.

The Glory of Magadha

In northern India, Xuanzang only saw monasteries in Magadha that still retained some of their old-time magnificence. The Gupta Empire was in decline, although a touch of its afterglow lingered in Harshavardhana's smaller empire in the East. Xuanzang praised Harshavardhana's justice and generosity. In the West, Buddhism is shown only in shreds and patches. At the time of Xuanzang, three of the grandest monastic establishments in Magadha were the Tilodaka Sangharama, the Mahabodhi Sangharama, and the Nalanda Mahavihara. They were not far from each other, all located in a cross-section of the modern state of Bihar. The Magadha of Fa-hien's time was a prosperous place. The towns of this country were especially large and the people were rich, thriving and virtuous.[16] The elaborate rituals he observed here perhaps signify prosperity and religiosity. Fa-hien describes a procession of images that took place every year on the eighth day of the second month. For this occasion, the people constructed a four-wheeled chariot and erected a five-storied tower made of bamboo on top of it. The entire edifice, which looked like a pagoda, was supported by a central post about 20 feet high, resembling a large spear with three points. This structure was then covered with fine white linen and painted with all kinds of vibrantly coloured images. Figures of all the *devas* (deities) were made and decorated with gold, silver and coloured glass. These were then placed under canopies of embroidered silk. Niches were constructed in the four corners of the chariot that served as shrines in which figures of the Buddha were placed in a sitting posture, with bodhisattvas (those on the path to Buddhahood) standing in attendance. Around twenty differently decorated chariots were thus readied.

On the day of the procession, the priests and the ordinary people assembled in large numbers. The priests offered flowers and incense in religious worship. The brahmacharis, the sons and disciples of the Brahmins, came forth to salute the Buddha. One after the other, the chariots were wheeled into the city and positioned at vantage points. All night, people lit lamps, played games, enjoyed various sources of amusement and made religious offerings. The ceremony resembled the procession of the chariot of Jagannath at Puri in Orissa.

---

[16]Ibid., 106.

People came from far and wide to attend this event. The nobles and landowners founded hospitals in the city, where the poor, destitute and diseased could find refuge. Physicians examined them and, according to their illness, ordered food and drink for them and gave them medicine or decoctions to ease their suffering.

Perceptions of the Pre-Nalanda Era

Xuanzang studied Buddhism for five years at Nalanda Mahavihara and gave a detailed history. On the other hand, Fa-hien does not even mention the university, despite describing places in its vicinity in detail. This implies that perhaps there was no Nalanda in Fa-hein's time; the university probably came into existence sometime in the fifth or sixth century—after Fa-hien and before Xuanzang. It has also been surmised that Fa-hien did not actually visit Nalanda. This seems strange because, even if the university was not established, the place was quite important as a monastery, with the Buddha himself having been there.

(The travellers) went on from this to the south-east for nine yojanas [a unit of measurement equal to about thirteen kilometres] and came to a small solitary rocky hill, at the head or end of which was an apartment of stone, facing south—the place where the Buddha sat, when Śakra, the Ruler of the devas, brought the deva-musician, Pañcha (śikha), to please him by playing on his lute. Śakra then asked the Buddha about forty-two subjects, tracing (the questions) one by one on the rock with his finger. The imprints are still there; and here also there is a monastery.

A yojana southwest from this place brought them to the village Nâla, where Sâriputtra was born, and to which also he returned, and attained here his parinirvâna.[17]

---

[17]Faxian, *A Record of Buddhistic Kingdoms being an account by The Chinese*

Scholars have also noted that Fa-hien confused the places he visited with those he had heard about in his account. This may have been because Fa-hien was the first Chinese pilgrim to travel to India and spent less time there than Xuanzang. Since Fa-hien was more interested in describing religious ceremonies, local myths and legends—accuracy of detail was probably not his top priority.

The city of Vaishali is about three hours' drive from modern Patna. It was the first place Fa-hien visited in modern Bihar. He saw the Great Forest Vihara, north of Vaishali, where he found a two-storey tower that the Buddha is said to have once occupied. This was built beside a tank known as Markata-hrda (literally monkey's heart) or 'monkey tank'. He also visited the ruins of a vihara about five or six kilometers south of the city. This vihara was in the mango orchard of Amradarika or the famous courtesan Ambapali (popularly known as Amrapali). She presented this mango orchard to the Buddha as a place for him to rest. The vihara was erected by Jivakarma, a physician who invited the Buddha and his 1,250 disciples to receive it as his offering. The Buddha honoured Ambapali by accepting her invitation to a feast at her home, after which he received the mango orchard and her palace and other possessions for the sangha. Ambapali herself became his disciple and achieved the position of an arhat.

When the Buddha was about to enter nirvana, he left Vaishali. He addressed his followers one last time, telling them that he would leave his body after he had performed the last religious act of his earthly life. The people built a stupa to mark the critical spot. According to a tradition, supported by the *Mahaparinirvana Sutra*, when the Buddha told his primary disciple, Ananda, that he would enter nirvana at the end of three months, Ananda did not understand that he should request the Buddha to remain in

---

Monk Fa-hien of His Travels in India and Ceylon (A.D. 399–414), James Legge (trans.), Oxford, Clarendon Press, 1886, pp. 80–81.

the world for the good of the people. The implication is that if Ananda had implored the Buddha to stay in the world, he would have lived on. However, it is said that Ananda was distraught because he was very devoted to the Buddha. Besides, he had not yet attained enlightenment and felt forlorn as he did not know the way forward without the Buddha. The Buddha had to counsel Ananda that he would soon attain enlightenment as his mind was so developed and he was in constant proximity to the Buddha. On Ananda's lament about what he would do after his death, the Buddha advised him to be a refuge for himself.

Vaishali was also the venue of the second Buddhist Council that sought to correct certain errors that had crept into the *Vinaya* a century after the Buddha's death. Buddhist monks were violating the rules of the Dharma and citing the *Vinaya* in their defence. This prompted the arhats and orthodox bhikkus to convene the second council, which was attended by over 700 monks. They breathed new life into the *Vinaya*, erecting a commemorative tower.

Fa-hien next came to Pataliputra (now Patna), the capital of King Ashoka. Little remains today of the city described by Fa-hien. In the middle of the city was the royal palace—he was so awestruck by its magnificence that he wrote that the walls, doors and sculpted towers, carved out of massive stones, could not have been human work. He concludes that King Ashoka must have commissioned genii or demons for the arduous task. He alludes to the myth that the younger brother of King Ashoka, Mahindra, having achieved the dignity of an arhat, habitually resided on the mountain of Gridhrakuta, finding his greatest joy in silent contemplation. The king had great regard and reverence for him and requested him to come to his house to receive his religious offerings. However, Mahindra was so happy with his tranquil life on the mountain that he declined the invitation.

The king then tried to persuade him by promising to build a hill for him within the city. He then invited the genii to a feast the following day, but they had to bring their own seats as he had no seats fit for their use. The next morning, all the great genii came, each bringing a great stone, four or five paces square. Immediately after the feast, King Ashoka asked the genii to pile up the great stones they had brought to make a mountain of them. At the base of this mountain, with five great square stones, they made a rock chamber about 35 feet long, 22 feet wide and 11 feet tall.

Fa-hien makes a similar assertion when he says that King Ashoka destroyed seven of the eight original stupas built on the relics of the Buddha that had been distributed after his funeral, but then proceeded to construct 84,000 stupas.

The first was the great tower, which, says Fa-hien, is about 3 li (about 1.5 kilometres) south of the city. In front of it was an impression of the Buddha's foot, over which a vihara was built with the gate facing north. To the south was a stone pillar, about 18 feet in girth and 35 feet or so in height. Engraved on the surface of this pillar was: 'King Asôka presented the whole of Jambudwîpa to the priests of the Four Quarters, and redeemed it again with money, and this he did four times.'[18] At the time of Xuanzang's visit, this tower was in ruins. About 300–400 paces north of it was Ashoka's birthplace and residence, where he is said to have built the city of Ni-lai or the town of Nala, in the midst of which he erected a stone pillar about 35 feet high, on the top of which he placed the figure of a lion. On the pillar was engraved a historical record giving an account of the successive events related to the city of Ni-lai with the corresponding dates.

In this city of Pataliputra, says Fa-hien, there once lived a learned Brahmin named Manjushri, a Mahayana Buddhist. The great shamans of the country and all the bhikkus practising Mahayana Buddhism revered him. The king of the country

---

[18]Fa-hsien, Faxian, *Travels of Fa-hian and Sung-yan Buddhist Pilgrims from China to India (400 A.D. and 518 A.D.)*, Samuel Beal and Susil Gupta (trans.), London, 1964, pp. 108–109.

honoured and respected him as his religious superior to such a great extent that he dared not sit in his presence when he wanted to greet him. Also, if the king took him by the hand of affection, the Brahmin immediately washed himself from head to toe. For about 50 years, the country looked up to him and placed its trust in him alone. This Brahmin extended the influence of the law of the Buddha so significantly that other religions could not make any inroads.

By the side of the tower of King Ashoka was a very elegant and imposing sangharama belonging to the Mahayana school of Buddhism. Manjushri is said to have lived there. There was also a temple of Hinayana Buddhism there. Together, they housed around 600 to 700 priests. An institution of learning was attached to the temple, where eminent shramanas from all parts of the world existed. Scholars seeking instruction flocked to this place.[19]

Discovery of Nalandagram and Rajagriha

Approximately 120 kilometres southeast of Pataliputra, Fa-hien came to a small rocky hill, on top of which was a stone cell facing the south. Xuanzang mentions this isolated rock as well. There is also a sangharama here near the village of Na-lo, otherwise called Nalandagram. It was near this village, which has been identified with the present Baragaon or Baragong or Viharagram, that the celebrated convent of Nalanda was constructed. Xuanzang lived in this magnificent establishment for five years. He makes Nalandagram the birthplace of Maudgalyayana or Mogalan and speaks of a country, or town, called Kalapinaka, which was the birthplace of Sariputra. In a subsequent account, Xuanzang speaks of a village called Kulika, as the birthplace of Mogalan.

---

[19]Faxian, *A Record of Buddhistic Kingdoms being an account by The Chinese Monk Fa-Hien A.D. 399-414, in Search of the Buddhist Books of Discipline*, James Legge (trans.), Oxford, Clarendon Press, 1886, p. 78.

Therefore, Kulika and Nalandagram must be different names of the same place. Sariputra was born in Rajagriha or Rajgir, which Xuanzang also calls Kalapinaka. Fa-hien probably confused the birthplace of Sariputra with that of Maudgalyayana. In any case, the two were contemporaries from neighbouring villages and childhood friends. Both were Vedic scholars, but its teachings did not give them a satisfactory answer to the truth. They became spiritual wanderers until they came across the Buddha's teachings, became ordained monks, and rose to be among the closest disciples of the Buddha. Maudgalyayana is said to have attained enlightenment shortly afterward. Sariputra returned to Nalandagram to enter nirvana, where a stupa was erected. According to Buddhist texts, his remains were enshrined in Jetavana, but subsequent archaeological findings suggest they were redistributed across the Indian subcontinent by various kings.

Going west for about 13 kilometres, Fa-hien arrived at the New Rajagriha, so called to distinguish it from the old town of the same name. It is said to have been built by King Shrenika or Bimbisara, the father of King Ajatashatru. In an account of the place, the Archaeological Survey of India gives the site's radius as somewhat less than two to three kilometres; it was built in the form of an irregular pentagon, with one long and four shorter ones. It is an important town in Buddhist history and close to the place of the Buddha's complete inspiration. At present, there is a village on this site retaining the name Rajgir, about 15 kilometres southwest of the town of Behar. Fa-hien found two sangharamas here. Nearby, about 300 paces away, he came to a tall and imposing tower or stupa raised by King Ajatashatru over his share of the Buddha's relics. After the Buddha's funeral, there were several claimants to his relics. The most authentic source of the events after the Buddha's death is to be found in the *Mahaparinirvana Sutra*. Initially, his relics were only intended for his clan, the Shakyas. However, the Mallas (the ruling clan) of Kushinagara, where he died, wanted to keep them for themselves. A war was imminent as chiefs of seven other clans got ready to fight the Mallas for the possession of the relics. They were saved by the intervention of the Brahmin Drona, who said:

One word from me, I beg you, sirs, to hear!
Our Buddha taught us ever to forbear;
Unseemly would it be should strife arise
And war and bloodshed, over the custody
Of his remains, who was the best of men!
Let us all, sirs, in friendliness, agree
To share eight portions—so that far and wide
Stupas may rise, and seeing them, mankind
Faith in the All-Enlightened One will find![20]

They all assented, and so Drona divided the relics into eight parts and kept the pot for himself. Thus, the Buddha's remains were shared by Ajatashatru, King of Magadha, Licchavis of Vaishali, Shakyas of Kapilavastu, Bulis of Allakappa, Koliyas of Ramagrama, Mallas of Pava, the Mallas of Kushinagara, and a Brahmin of Vethadipa. The last one is a mystery, and there is no mention of him in the *Tripitaka*. Bhante Dhammika, an Australian Buddhist monk, suggests that he was from a place now called Jahangira, an island formed by rocks in the middle of the river Ganga, at Sultanganj in Bihar. He arrived at this conclusion by basing his findings on the etymology of Vethadipa. *Vetha* in Pali means to be enclosed or enveloped; *dipa* means either a lamp or an island. The ocean would be about 700 kilometres from where the Buddha lived, therefore he thought it was unlikely that the reference would be to an island. Also, there was no island on the Yamuna but there was a permanent island on the Ganga—Jahangira at Sultanganj. Being only about 200 kilometres from Patna, this was the most likely place for

[20]*Maha-parinibbana Sutta: Last Days of the Buddha,* Sister Vajira and Francis Story (trans.), Buddhist Publication Society, Ceylon, May 1961, pp. 111-112.

Vethadipa. Further, although a modern temple now stands there, statues of the Buddha have been found below it, showing that it was a Buddhist island at one time. Xuanzang also mentions that he spent a year studying there with two famous pandits, Tathagatagupta and Shantisimha. This shows that it must have been a Buddhist centre of considerable importance. Over time, it had to share its space with Hindu temples, but perhaps this place holds the key to the Brahmin of Vethadipa.

Leaving the city's south side and proceeding about two kilometres, Fa-hien entered a valley between five hills. These hills surround the valley like the walls of a town. This is the site of the old town of King Bimbisara. It is about 2.5 to 3 kilometres from east to west, and 3.5 to 4 kilometres from north to south. It is said that Sariputra and Mogalan first met the Buddha's disciple, Ashvajit, here and converted to Buddhism. This city is the old Rajagriha or Kusagarapura. Xuanzang also speaks of a city encompassed by hills. These hills represent a circuit of about 10 kilometres.

Many attempts were made here on the Buddha's life, which Fa-hien recounts. It is said that a Niragrantha or a Digambar Jain ascetic named Srigupta invited the Buddha to a meal, which he poisoned. He also made a fire pit and covered it lightly. His aim was to make the Buddha fall into the pit, but instead, the fire was extinguished as the Buddha approached and the pit filled with water. Fa-hien also talks of where King Ajatashatru desired to destroy the Buddha by intoxicating a black elephant. This crime, however, is generally ascribed to Devadatta (Buddha's brother-in-law and greatest enemy) and not to Ajatashatru.

From the valley, skirting the mountains along the south-eastern slope for about 7.5 kilometres, Fa-hien arrived at Gridhrakuta Mountain. This is the Vulture Peak, the Buddha's favourite place for meditation. About 1.5 kilometres from the top of the mountain was a stone cavern facing south. It was here that the Buddha sat in profound meditation. Some 30 paces to the northwest was another stone cell where Ananda practised meditation.

The Legend of Kalanda

Returning to the new city, after passing through the old town and walking about 300 paces northwards, on the west side of the road, Fa-hien came to the Kalandavenouvana Vihara or the vihara in the bamboo garden of Kalanda. According to legend, a squirrel or *kalanda* saved the life of the king of Vaishali, who was asleep in this forest, by chirping in his ear when a snake approached. This prompted him to decree that no one should kill a squirrel in his domain as it would mean death and that the squirrels in that garden should be fed regularly. A wealthy householder living in this neighbourhood was given the name Kalanda, and he built the vihara and presented it to the Buddha. Some of the Buddha's most celebrated discourses were delivered here. In another version, King Bimbisara gave it to the Buddha. In Fa-hien's time, the vihara still existed, and the congregation of priests swept and watered it. About a kilometre north of the vihara was a *shamshana*, a cremation ground. Skirting the southern hill and 300 paces westwards, Fa-hien found a stone cell, the Pipal Cave, where the Buddha is said to have sat in deep meditation after his midday meal. About two or three kilometres further on, in the northern shadow of the mountain, there was another stone cave, Chetiwas. Xuanzang also describes this cave as the Sattapani (or Saptaparni) Cave, where the first great Buddhist assembly was held immediately after the Buddha's nirvana.

500 arhats assembled here to arrange the collection of the Buddha's teachings at a time when the books were ordinarily recited. Three vacant seats were specially prepared and adorned. The left one was for Sariputra and the right one was for Maudgalyayana, but it is said that the assembly was yet short of one arhat to reach 500. Mahakashyapa, one of the chief disciples,

was just taking his seat to preside over the assembly. Ananda stood outside the gate, unable to find admission because he had not yet found enlightenment. However, he attained it just then, remembering that the Buddha had told him to be his refuge. Ananda played a crucial role in the assembly by reciting the Buddha's teachings, which were accepted as he was considered the most knowledgeable on the matter because of his close and constant proximity to the Buddha. According to Fa-hien, a tower had been erected at this place to mark the event. Still skirting the mountain, he saw many other stone cells used by the arhats for meditation. Leaving the old city and going northeast for about a kilometre and a half, he arrived at Devadatta's stone cell. Fifty paces away was a tremendous square black stone, perhaps a reminder of the rock that Devadatta had hurled at the Buddha to kill him.

About 68 kilometres west of Rajagriha, Fa-hien came to the town of Gaya, which he found desolate and deserted. This is where the Buddha is said to have attained complete enlightenment. It is usually said that there are two Gayas—Buddha Gaya or Bodhgaya and the town of Gaya. Buddha Gaya is about six miles north of Gaya, which seems to be the site of the ruins of numerous sacred buildings. But Fa-hien visited the town of Gaya, which he also found deserted. About 10 kilometres south of Gaya, he arrived at a wooded place where the Buddha is said to have spent six years in self-imposed austerity in his quest for enlightenment. From here, Fa-hien proceeded for about 1.5 kilometres westwards and reached Supratishtita, where, when the Buddha went into the water to bathe, he is said to have been helped out of the water by a deva who held out a tree branch to him. Legend has it that while the Buddha was bathing in the river Niranjana, all the devas waited on him with flowers and perfumes, which they threw into the midst of the river. After he had bathed, a tree deva held down a branch as if stretching out a hand to assist him in coming out of the water.

About a kilometre further, Fa-hien came to the place where the village girls gave milk and rice to the Buddha. There are two versions of this legend. One is that Sujata offered milk and rice to the Buddha while her two daughters offered the rice; the other is that it was provided by her two daughters, Nanda and Nandabala, or Trapusha and Bhallika. According to Fa-hien, about two li or a mile north is where the Buddha, seated on a stone under a great tree and facing east, ate rice and milk. According to him, the stone was approximately six square feet in measurement, and both the stone and the tree still existed despite a lapse of several centuries.

The Buddha and the Celestials

About seven kilometres to the northeast, Fa-hien saw a natural cave where the Buddha had sat cross-legged facing west. He reflected that if he wanted to arrive at the state of perfect wisdom, a spiritual manifestation had to occur. Immediately, the shadow of the Buddha, about three feet long, appeared on the stone. This shadow, according to Fa-hien, was distinctly visible. The heavens and the earth shook so wildly that all the devas who resided in the heavens cried out and said that this was not the place appointed for the Buddhas—of the past or those to come—to attain perfect wisdom. That place was six to seven kilometres southwest towards a pipal tree (*Ficus religiosa* or sacred fig). Having thus spoken, the devas led the way, singing for the Buddha to follow. The Buddha rose and walked after them. When they had gone 30 paces, the devas presented the Buddha with the grass mat of Shanti. The reference is to the Brahmin called Shanti, who gave the Buddha eight bundles of *kusha* grass because he knew it would be needed. The Buddha, arriving at the pipal tree, spread the mat of Shanti under it and sat down facing east. Five hundred bluebirds flew towards him and took off after encircling him three times in flight. Then the Mara, or the celestial demon king, dispatched three pleasure girls from the northern quarter to seduce him and assailed him from the south likewise. The Buddha struck his toe against the earth, scattering the whole army of Mara, and the three women were turned into hags.

Men erected stupas and placed figures of the Buddha where he mortified himself for six years by practising severe austerities and on each spot subsequently mentioned. Having attained supreme wisdom, the Buddha sat, contemplating, under the tree for seven days, experiencing the joys of emancipation. Here, too, a stupa had been raised. To mark the place where he walked for seven days under the pipal tree, from east to west, says Fa-hien, the devas created a hall of seven precious substances and worshipped the Buddha for seven days. A stupa marked this place as well as where the blind dragon Manlun encircled the Buddha for seven days as a token of respect; where the Buddha sat on a square stone under a Nyagrodha tree facing east and received the respectful salutation of Brahma; where the four celestial kings who rule over the four quarters, the four Buddhist gods said to originate from the Hindu concept of *lokapalas*—each guarding a cardinal direction—respectfully offered him his alms bowl; where the 500 merchants presented him with wheat and honey; and where he converted the two Kashyapa brothers, each at the head of 1,000 disciples.

At the place where the Buddha arrived at perfect wisdom, Fa-hien found three functioning sangharamas with resident monks. People supplied them with all the necessities, so they had enough and lacked nothing. They scrupulously observed the rules of the *Vinaya* concerning decorum and conformed to the regulations established by the Buddha when he was in the world. These are related to sitting down, rising, entering the assembly, and the like. Four great pagodas were erected at the place in Lumbini where the Buddha was born, a UNESCO World Heritage site, the Mahabodhi Temple in Bodhgaya, where he obtained emancipation, another World Heritage Site, the Dhamekh Stupa in Sarnath, where he began preaching, and the Ramabhar Stupa in Kushinagar where he entered nirvana. These sites have always been taken together and form a significant cluster.

Quest for the Scriptures

Fa-hien once again returned to Pataliputra. His purpose in coming to India was to seek copies of the *Vinaya Pitaka*. Throughout northern India, the various masters still relied mainly on the oral tradition for their knowledge of the precepts and for transmitting this knowledge to their disciples, having no written texts. This is an esstential statement by Fa-hien, for it shows that even during his time, Buddhist doctrine had been preserved in the different central establishments principally as oral teachings. Perhaps this accounts, to a certain extent, for the springing up of various schools of Buddhism. In general, each of the 18 sects has its superiority, but they are united in dependence on the great refuge found in the Buddha, Dhamma and sangha. They differ in some minor details of faith and their exact attention to some matters of practice.

Fa-hien had come even so far as Middle India, but his purpose had not been achieved. However, in the sangharama of the Mahayana at Patna, he obtained a copy of the precepts: the collection used by the Mahasanghika school (an early Buddhist school). This was supposedly used in the first great assemply of monks. The Jetavana Vihara claimed that this was originally their copy, by which they may have meant that this school originated from them. In any case, this collection is generally regarded as the most correct and complete version of the precepts. Further, Fa-hien obtained one copy of the *Abhidhamma* comprising about 7,000 *gatha*s (verses), which he either transcribed himself or had one of the priests copy for him. This was used by the assembly of the Sarvastivada school (an early school established during the reign of King Ashoka). He also obtained an imperfect copy of the *Abhidhamma*, which included about 6,000 *gatha*s and a collection of sutras in their abbreviated form, consisting of 2,500 verses. Further, he found an expanded volume of the *Parinirvana Sutra*, containing about 5,000 verses. He also procured a copy of the *Abhidhamma*, according to the Mahasanghika school. Hence, Fa-hien stayed here for three years, learning to read Sanskrit books, converse in this language, and copy the precepts.

Following down the river Ganga for about 240 kilometres in an easterly direction, Fa-hien came to the southern shore of the great kingdom of Champa. Champa, or Champapuri, was the name of the ancient capital of a country called Angadesha. In the epic Mahabharata, Karna was made the king of Anga, also called Karnapura. The place corresponds with the present Bhagalpura. Xuanzang also came here and spoke of the number of heretical sects intermingled in this place. Buddhism began getting corrupted early in this part of India as local superstitions crept in. Stupas had been erected where the Buddha once dwelt and where he moved to and fro for exercise.

From here, Fa-hien continued to travel eastward until he arrived at the port of Tamralipta, a journey of about 800 kilometres. From this port, near the mouth of the river Hoogly, there was extensive traffic with Sinhala and the southern coasts of India. Fa-hien found 24 sanghramas here with resident priests who respected the law of the Buddha. Fa-hien stayed here for two years, writing copies of the sacred books and taking impressions of the figures used in worship. He then boarded a great merchant ship, and setting to sea, sailed for 14 days and nights in a south-westerly direction—catching the first fair winds of winter—to arrive at the country of the Lions, or Sinhala (Ceylon). Thus, Fa-hien's journey to India ended.

The Return

Fa-hien stayed in Ceylon for two years and then wanted to return to China, as several years had passed since he left his own country.

He boarded a ship that was driven to Java by a storm. From there, he boarded another ship to Canton but was once again caught in a storm that drove him to the Shandong Peninsula in eastern China. By this time, he had spent over 200 days at sea, and his journey from start to finish took just a little over 12 years.

3

In Search of the Higher Truth: The Odyssey of Xuanzang

Just over two centuries after Fa-hien's return to his homeland, Xuanzang, a brilliant scholar from China, came to India and specifically to Nalanda in search of a distinguished and authentic teacher to gain greater clarity on the texts of the Yogachara school of Buddhism, one of the two major schools of Indian Mahayana Buddhist thought. Xuanzang is perhaps the best-known Chinese scholar of Nalanda, and the monument dedicated to him near the archaeological site bears witness to this.

He was the bridge between the two ancient civilizations of China and India and made an unparalleled contribution to Buddhist literature in China. The zeal of the students of the time, who were in search of the best teachers and the superior education they could provide, is embodied in the 10,000-mile journey Xuanzang undertook on foot and on horseback to reach the historic University of Nalanda.

In 1942, the burial chamber of an ancient Buddhist pagoda was discovered during the construction of an Inari Shinto shrine just outside of Nanjing's southern gate in the Jiangsu province of China. A stone sarcophagus with two boxes was found inside. There were inscriptions on the walls of the sarcophagus, one dating to the eleventh century and the other to the fourteenth century. This led to the bone in the box being identified as a fragment of

Xuanzang's skull. Part of this shard was given to the then Indian prime minister Jawaharlal Nehru by the Chinese government of Zhou Enlai, together with a biography of Xuanzang, a copy of his book on his journey to India, and 1,335 sutra volumes of his translated works. These were handed over by His Holiness the Dalai Lama on behalf of the Chinese government in 1957.

Xuanzang's journey is the stuff legends are made of. The same Xuanzang who crept away like a thief from his country returned to a king's welcome. While his epic journey is the subject of many books, it is also the theme of one of China's four great classic novels. Written by Wu Chang'en and published in the sixteenth century, its abridged English translation by Arthur Waley, titled *Monkey*, is well-known in English-speaking countries. Xuanzang recorded his journey with great accuracy at the behest of the emperor in the *Great Tang Records on the Western Regions*. This was the document that Alexander Cunningham used to excavate the places mentioned by Xuanzang. Xuanzang himself is hardly mentioned in this text. We must turn to Hui Li, a contemporary biographer of Xuanzang, to put flesh and blood into the details of the journey and to see Xuanzang as a person.

Despite his young age, Xuanzang was already an established scholar and a venerated priest in China when he chose to undertake his arduous journey to India. His illustrious predecessor, Fa-hien, visited India at the end of the fourth and beginning of the fifth century but did not leave an account as detailed as Xuanzang's. Separated by more than a century, a comparison between the two accounts shows the changing fortunes of Buddhism in his land. Xuanzang's dedication to learning and spiritual growth inspired more monks to follow his example. His most notable follower was I-Ching, who wrote a detailed record of Buddhist practices in India and the lives of the Chinese monks who came to India during the seventh century.

Background

The sixth century was a time of great confusion in China. The Sui dynasty had ended and the Tang Dynasty would soon replace it. The Duke of Tang declared Chang'an as his capital. Hui Li eloquently describes the political confusion and mayhem in Chang'an, where Xuanzang and his brother took refuge after fleeing Luoyang. They first went to Sichuan, where they found some teachers from their old convent in Chengdu and stayed there for a few years. Here, Xuanzang met the monk Teo-Chi, who had learnt from Ching-Sung, whose teacher had been the Indian monk, Paramartha. Xuanzang was still searching for a significant *shastra* (scripture) belonging to the Yogachara school of Buddhism. His interest was in the nature of consciousness. For example, he wanted to study whether human consciousness was fundamentally pure or impure. He was attracted to Buddhist texts after the second century CE, as these had begun to emphasise the nature of consciousness.

From Sichuan, Xuanzang travelled, preached, studied with the Chinese masters of the time, and debated with his contemporary scholars. His was a prodigious mind. It is said that he understood a book after hearing it only once, and after the second hearing, he needed no further instruction. Priests were astonished at the clarity and precision of his explanations and listened to him with rapt attention. The foundations of his renown were laid when he was a mere 13-year-old child. He earned praise wherever he went, but in 625 CE, he and his brother were forced to leave the Tsing-tu Temple, where they lived because of the widespread unrest at the end of the Sui Dynasty and seek refuge in the city of Shing-tu in Sz'chuen province. He was ordained here when he was 20 years old.[21]

---

[21]Xuanzang, *Si-yu-ki: Buddhist Records of the Western World*, Samuel Beal (trans.), Routledge, California, 2008, p. xviii.

Xuanzang returned to Chang'an and started to live at Mahabodhi Monastery or sangharama. The unrest gradually settled, and Li Shimin became the new emperor of the Tang Dynasty, calling himself Tang Taizong, or Taizong of Tang. What would later be perceived as the golden age of China began under the Tangs, even though the monks were initially apprehensive about the situation of Buddhism, as the Tang clan came from a Taoist lineage.

Xuanzang clearly wanted to translate the *Yogacharabhumi-Shastra*, and for that, he would travel to India. He had before him the examples of Fa-hien and Chi-yen, who had first come to India in search of the Dharma. Their efforts, Xuanzang thought, would not be in vain. As he went about his tasks at the monastery, he constantly thought of Fa-hien, Sung-yun, and Hui Sheng, the monks who had visited India before him, for he felt it was his duty to follow in their footsteps.

The Secret Departure

While Emperor Taizong of Tang sat firmly on the throne, he had trouble with the Turks. It was the age-old clash between the farming, settled Han Chinese and the nomadic horsemen who wandered around the steppes of Mongolia and northern Central Asia. Hence, Taizong was vigilant about the borders and banned all foreign travel. Xuanzang, too, was denied permission to travel. However, he was determined to follow in the footsteps of his predecessors and secretly set off from Xian—the starting point of the Silk Road—on a moonless autumn night in 627 CE. Xuanzang headed towards Liangzhou, where a religious conference was taking place. Since he already had an excellent reputation, he was given a place of honour at the conference. As he was far away from the capital, Xuanzang perhaps let his guard down and talked about his forthcoming travel to India more openly. Word reached Li Dahang, the governor of Liangzhou, who summoned Xuanzang to warn him of the dangers of the journey and to strictly forbid him from travelling, as the emperor had prohibited it.

Xuanzang was not deterred. Late that night, he was secretly escorted by Hwui-Lin and Taou-Ching, two disciples of Hwui-Wei, a monk who was an admirer of Xuanzang. They left Liangzhou, hid during the day in wilder mountain regions to avoid detection, and travelled at night. Eventually, they arrived at the garrison town of Kwachow, the western edge of the modern Gansu province of China. To its north was the Badain Desert, and to the south were the snow-covered foothills of the Qinhan Mountains. The journey so far had been exhausting; his feet were calloused as his horse had died on the way.

The news of Xuanzang's journey had reached To-Kiu, the governor of Kwa Chow, who was delighted to receive him and his two companions. He provided them with plenty of provisions but also cautioned him about the greater perils that lay ahead. He mapped out the route that Xuanzang would take. He had to travel 50 li, or about 25 kilometres (2 li equalled 1 kilometre) to the north when he would come to the Hulu River, which was wide in the lower section and narrower upstream. The water was choppy, making it very difficult to ferry across. In the upper part was the Jade Gate barrier, and beyond the barrier were five watchtowers 50 kilometres apart. This area had nothing—no food, water or even grass. There was not a single drop of water to be found between the last two watchtowers. Bones of animals and men lay strewn, bringing home a grim realization of what could befall Xuanzang and his convoy. Beyond the watchtowers was the Mo-Kia-Yen Desert.

The Perils of the Lone Traveller

The two disciples were dismayed by the rigours of the journey and left. Xuanzang, however, met Pan-to, a Mongolian horseman. Pan-to asked Xuanzang if he could become the latter's lay disciple, to which Xuanzang agreed. Delighted, he presented him with cakes and fruit. Since he appeared to be a man of strong build and quick intelligence, Xuanzang told him about his upcoming travels and asked him for help. Pan-to readily agreed to accompany him and left Xuanzang only to return shortly after with an old man riding a lean red-haired horse. Pan-to assured the sceptical Xuanzang that this old man would be his best guide. The old man warned Xuanzang of the dangers ahead and parted ways with him, leaving behind the horse, which he said had made several journeys like the one Xuanzang was about to undertake.

Xuanzang and Pan-to travelled through the night. In the early hours of dawn, they reached a river they had to cross, and Pan-to chopped some wood to build a bridge. Having crossed the river, the tired but happy Xuanzang decided to rest. Xuanzang dreamt of Pan-to approaching him with a drawn knife. He prayed to Guanyin, the bodhisattva of compassion. More than a dream, it was Xuanzang's subconscious warning him of Pan-to's attempt to kill him. Xuanzang awoke with a start. He found his companion stealing towards him with the knife. Luckily, better sense prevailed and Pan-to retreated and went to sleep. The following day, realizing the rigours of the journey, Pan-to abandoned the monk like the others before him, and Xuanzang was left to face the desert alone.

Tricked by heat and light as he hazarded his way across, guided by heaps of bones and dried horse dung, Xuanzang experienced a mirage. He saw troops—hundreds of them, wrapped in fur and felt—advancing towards him. As they stopped, he saw camels and horses, standards and lances. He thought they were robbers, but they all vanished and reappeared as demons. About 40 kilometres later, Xuanzang reached the first watchtower.

Knowing that he was contravening the emperor's commands, Xuanzang hid from the guards. Finding water, he knelt to drink and wash himself. He wet a corner of his robe, wiped his neck, and filled his gourd container. Just then, an arrow whistled past him. He called out that he was a priest and should not be harmed.

Soldiers arrived and led him to their chief, Wang Siang. Having convinced Wang of his identity and his resolve to go to the West, he slept peacefully as Wang himself promised to show him the right way.

In the morning, after Xuanzang had eaten some food, Wang Siang provided him with water and cakes for his journey and accompanied him for about 5 kilometres. Then, pointing to the road ahead, he told Xuanzang to keep following it, as it would lead him to the fourth watchtower, where a man from his own family oversaw its gate. He would take care of Xuanzang.

Travelling from morning till night, Xuanzang came to the fourth watchtower. Fearing he might be detained, he decided to fetch some water and quietly go on. He had barely reached the water when an arrow flew towards him again. Turning around, he called out as he had earlier and went to the tower. The tower officer questioned Xuanzang, and he was warmly welcomed after giving Wang's message. He was given fodder for his horse and water in his bottle. The officer warned Xuanzang not to stop at the fifth tower, as the man there was rough, and some mishap might befall him. Instead, he advised him to walk 50 kilometres ahead, where he would come to the Ye-ma spring and could replenish his water.

Deserts, Mirages and Exhaustion

Xuanzang walked on through the Mo-Kia-Yen Desert; its old name was Sha-ho, or 'the river of sand', stretching for up to 400 kilometres. The sand was shifting and treacherous. It was one of the worst experiences of his journey, as the extremities of the desert caused him to see visions of goblins and demons. He continued, chanting mantras and praying to Guanyin. However, lost and confused, he wandered off the track and missed the Ye-ma spring, where he was supposed to fill his depleted water gourd. Worse still, as he lifted it to drink the last drops of water left in his receptacle, his horse stumbled, and the gourd fell from his hand. All the water poured out onto the hot sands of Mo-Kia-Yen. Frightened and helpless, he fell to the ground exhausted; he had to remind himself of his vow that he would not look back and continue until he reached his destination, even if it meant death. He resolutely continued to pray to Guanyin as he felt the hot tears of frustration and helplessness streaming down his face. For four nights and five days, Xuanzang could not find a drop of water to wet his throat. His stomach was wracked by burning heat, his skin blistered, and his lips cracked. His memory dissolved, and nothing was left save his resolve. He slid off his horse and collapsed in a crumpled heap onto the sand. Dizzy and faint, he prayed until night fell, and the stars rose. Suddenly, he felt a cool breeze fanning him, cold and refreshing like an icy bath. He sank into sleep and dreamt that a mighty beast was asking him why he was sleeping and not going ahead.

Xuanzang roused himself and mounted his horse. They had gone about five kilometres when his horse suddenly started on another way and could not be turned around. Exhausted, Xuanzang let the horse lead him. This was a fortuitous decision, as the canny horse had led its rider to an oasis. The monk and the horse were granted a reprieve, as they found life-restoring water and fresh grass. They stayed there for a day and replenished their bodies and stores of food and water, following which Xuanzang proceeded towards I-Gu.

Some Royal Help

Two days later, Xuanzang arrived in I-Gu, where he stopped at a temple and met three Chinese priests. One of them, an old man, ran out barefoot to greet him, and Xuanzang, recognizing a fellow Chinese, embraced him with tears in his eyes. The foreign priests and kings all came to pay him their respects. The king invited him to his house, where Xuanzang met the messengers of the king of Kau-Chang, Khio-wen-t'ai. On their return, the messengers informed their king about Xuanzang, who immediately sent a message ordering the king of I-Gu to send Xuanzang to him. Xuanzang respectfully declined but to no avail. He was obliged to go.

The king sent a cavalry of horses, officers and ministers to welcome him and accompany him to Kau-Chang. These were men who knew the shifting sands of the desert well. They led the monk for six days across ridges and dunes, over rocky patches filled with prickly grass, after which they reached Pih-Li, a city on the borders of Kau-Chang. It was past midnight when they arrived at the city gates. King Khio-wen-t'ai himself received Xuanzang. The queen and her attendants soon joined him. A devout Buddhist, the king was delighted to meet Xuanzang, seeing in this visit a rare opportunity for solace and guidance. The king kept the monk awake all night, conversing with him, until the latter begged for sleep.

Khio-wen-t'ai wanted Xuanzang to stay with him and not think of continuing his journey further. He tried to make him as comfortable as he could and sent a resident monk to persuade him to do so. He also summoned the 80-year-old Buddhist master Kwo-tong-wang and requested him to convince the monk to stay. This went on for ten days—the king begged Xuanzang on his knees to stay. When this had no effect, the king threatened force, but Xuanzang remained undeterred. He stopped eating and sat in complete silence for three days. The king, ashamed, agreed to let Xuanzang go on the condition that he would stay with him for three years on his way back. The monk agreed.

While the king prepared for Xuanzang's departure, the monk stayed for a month, expounding the Dharma. The king provided 100 ounces of gold, 30,000 pieces of silver, and 500 rolls of satin and taffeta to finance Xuanzang's journey back and forth. He also selected 30 horses and 24 of his best servants to accompany Xuanzang. He assigned Hun-Sin, an imperial official, to conduct him across the icy mountains to Khan Yeh Hu, who ruled over what is today known as Kyrgyzstan. Khio-wen-t'ai wrote 24 letters of introduction asking the rulers whom Xuanzang would encounter en route to provide him with relays of horses in their respective countries.

New Perils

On the day of departure, the king accompanied Xuanzang a short distance towards the kingdom of O-ki-ni, where the fountain of A-fu is situated on a sandy hillock. The water came from a hill halfway up. The story goes that once a band of several hundred merchants had finished their water supply in the middle of their journey. Exhausted and parched, they did not know what to do. Among them was a priest who had brought no provisions for himself but relied on alms from the rest. While the others were very anxious, the priest was serene. When asked what they should do, he advised the merchants to pray to the Buddha while he would climb the hill and cause the water to flow out. The water cascaded exactly as he promised after the traders had prayed to the Buddha and accepted the rules of moral obligation. Since then, the waters have continued to flow.

After spending the night by the fountain, Xuanzang rode over the Silver Mountain with his small band of travellers. The gorge was extremely steep. Rocky crags and grey slate rocks jutted right up to their faces. Just then, they were attacked by armed robbers, forcing the travellers to hand over everything they had, including food. Xuanzang then joined a band of 20 or 30 merchants, perhaps Central Asians, returning after a lucrative stop in Chang'an. But this move also did not provide any safety, as Xuanzang would later discover to his horror. They pitched their tents by a stream and slept for a while. The merchants woke up early and set off, hoping to get a head start on their trade, but when Xuanzang caught up with them later in the day, he was horrified to find their mangled bodies. Jewellery had been torn off their ears and their clothes ripped off. The sight made him sick.

Xuanzang's escorts decided they must all go to the safety of the city walls of O-ki-ni. Upon hearing of his arrival, the king of O-ki-ni rode out to meet Xuanzang and invited him to the palace as his guest. However, as this country had formerly been subjected to attacks from brigands from Kau-Chang, the king was unwilling to give them an escort for further travel. Xuanzang rested for a night, crossed a great river and a scenic valley, and finally arrived at the borders of the kingdom of Kiu-chi after travelling several hundred kilometres.

The king of Kiu-chi went to Xuanzang accompanied by a Buddhist priest, Mokshagupta, while thousands of priests waited at the city's eastern gate to welcome him in a pavilion they had especially erected for him; bands played in his honour. Kiu-chi was an ancient state and had been a part of King Ashoka's empire. He had instituted several Buddhist ceremonies there, which were still being performed. Xuanzang found Mokshagupta's knowledge superficial and tried to avoid him as much as possible to avoid conflict. However, Xuanzang was compelled to stay in Kui-chi for two months while waiting for the snowbound passes of Mount Ling to open. On the day of his departure, the king gave Xuanzang servants, camels and horses, had him attended by monks and amateurs, and personally accompanied him a good distance.

After a two-day journey through a small sandy desert, they arrived in Poh-luh-kia, where they stopped for a night. On the way, the caravan had stumbled upon a camp of 2,000 Turkish robbers and had had a narrow escape as they hid fearfully behind the rocks. The robbers were too busy arguing over the division of the spoils from the caravan they had pillaged earlier to rob them.

After another 150 kilometres, they crossed another desert and reached the very high, steep and dangerous Ling Mountain. Here, it snowed perpetually and the accumulated snow formed unrelenting glaciers. It was extremely challenging and risky to climb this mountain. Xuanzang prayed to Guanyin continuously as they crossed the mountain, but many men died because of the rugged terrain, starving or freezing to death in the seven days it took them to cross. There was no shelter or even a dry place. They had to hang their pots in the open and unroll their mats to sleep on the ice. Each morning, they counted the grey faces with frozen eyelashes who lay dead under their blankets, covered in a film of ice. Over 14 men died and had to be left behind. Many more oxen and horses perished. This experience was to haunt Xuanzang for the rest of his life. It taught him to be more careful with human and animal life, however strong his enthusiasm and determination may be.

After leaving the mountains, they arrived at the formidable Tsing Lake, whose waters were whipped into enormous waves by gusts of wind. Following its shores, they reached Su-yeh after walking about 250 kilometres. Here, they met the Khan of the Turks, Yeh-Hu, who was leaving on a hunting expedition. The Khan exuded power and opulence. He wore a robe of green satin and his long hair was tied back with a long silken band. He was surrounded by around 200 officers—all dressed in brocade— with braided hair. He was guarded by troops clothed in furs and garments made of finespun hair. They carried lances, bows and standards, and were mounted on camels and the finest horses.

The Khan asked Xuanzang to stay until he returned from his hunting expedition and directed one of his chief officers to conduct him to a large tent and see to his needs. These men were fire-worshippers, not followers of the Buddha. When the Khan returned a couple of days later, a feast was held in the monk's honour, at which the men ate and drank copiously. After the feast, the drinking continued, and in such an unpropitious environment, the Khan asked Xuanzang to expound his doctrines.

Despite the unusual setting, something must have made an impact. Perhaps it was the idea of a life beyond the barbarism they lived. The Khan accepted the moral precepts taught by Xuanzang and asked him to stay without continuing his journey. But when the Khan realized that the monk was determined to leave, he found a man who could speak fluent Chinese, who had lived in Chang'an for several years, to escort him to Kapisha. Moreover, the Khan gave Xuanzang red satin vestments and 50 pieces of silk and accompanied him for about 10 li.

Passing through Ping-yu, Taras, Poh-schwui, Kong-Yu and Nu-Chon-Kieu, Xuanzang came to Che-Sher. To its west, it bordered the Yeh-yeh River. He then travelled another 500 kilometres along the river and arrived at the kingdom of Su-tu-li-sse-na (Sutrishna). He then crossed another great desert to arrive at Sa-no-kien (Samarkand). Here, too, the king and his people were fire-worshippers. Although there were two religious shelters, no priests inhabited them. If a foreign priest tried to seek refuge there, he was chased away.

Initially, the king treated Xuanzang with disdain, but after an extensive discussion with him the following day, he became his disciple. When Xuanzang went to worship at the temple with his disciples, some people tried to chase them away. The king was infuriated and ordered their hands to be cut off. They were saved because of Xuanzang's intervention, and their sentence was reduced to exile. This earned him the people's respect. Xuanzang called a large assembly and accepted many of them as priests, establishing them in the convents.

Resuming his journey, Xuanzang finally arrived at Kesh, from where he had to return to the mountains. The road was deep and dangerous, barely wide enough at some places for men to pass in a single file. There were no plants or water. After about 500 kilometres, Xuanzang arrived at the Silk Road's Iron Gate Pass. The precipices were perpendicular, like walls on either side, leaving only a narrow passage. Attached to these was a folding iron gate with many cast-iron bells suspended from it. It was meant to serve as a barrier against the advance of the Turks.

Passing through the gates, they arrived at Tu-ho-lo and travelled several hundred kilometres to reach and cross the river Oxus, after which they entered the kingdom of Hwo. This was the residence of Khan Yeh Hu, who was married to Kau-Chang's sister. He met Xuanzang when he learnt he had carried letters from Kau-Chang for him and his wife. However, his wife had already died and he was very sick. Gradually, he recovered and married his wife's sister. But she conspired with her dead sister's son to poison the king. The nephew, being the heir, violently seized the throne and married his father's widow. As the king's funeral ceremony was being carried out, Xuanzang had to stay in this kingdom for over a month.

There he met a monk called Ta-mo-sang-kia or Dharmasinha, who had travelled to India and received instruction there. He was so learned that the scholars hesitated to debate with him. However, Xuanzang bested him. By this time, the new king had established his government. Xuanzang sought him out and requested him for official envoys and horses for his onward journey. The king asked Xuanzang to visit Bactra or Balkh on his way as it was home to so many sacred sites that it was known as Little Rajagriha. Since priests were visiting from Bactra, Xuanzang agreed to accompany them. On arriving, the place seemed barren to him, but it had about a 100 sangharamas with 3,000 priests.

Accompanied by a monk named Pragyakara, whom he had met on the way, Xuanzang left Balkh and came to the kingdom of Kie-chi. They entered the snowy Hindu Kush mountains from the southeast of this kingdom. Travelling another 300 kilometres, they entered the kingdom of Bamiyan. Nestled amid high mountains, its winding and crooked paths were extremely dangerous. The main town had about ten religious foundations with thousands of priests. The king of Bamiyan came out to meet him and escorted him to his palace. There, he met two priests, Aryadesa and Aryasena, who were full of admiration for him. They took him from place to place and eventually to the two awe-inspiring statues of the Buddha, one of which was 100 feet high while the other reached 150 feet.

After about 15 days, Xuanzang left Bamiyan, but on the second day of the journey, he encountered a snowstorm and lost his way. Coming to a small sandy hillock, he met some hunters who gave him directions. He made his way through Gandhara, across the Indus River and reached the Hunza Valley. He walked past rock carvings on the cliff walls and passed over narrow iron bridges that swayed in the wind, linking one mountain flank to another.

Xuanzang's Arrival in Kashmir

Xuanzang followed the course of the Jhelum River, crossed the Baramulla Pass and finally reached the western entrance to the kingdom of Kashmir. It was the end of the year 628 CE. He had been on the road for a year and had covered 13,800 li (6,900 kilometres).

When the news reached the palace, the king's mother and younger brother rushed to the borders in chariots to greet the priest from China. He was shown monasteries on the way and taken to the establishment at Hushkara, where Kashmiri monks looked after him for the night. Hushkara housed 100 religious centres with 5,000 priests. There were also four magnificent stupas built by King Ashoka. King Durlabhavardhana, who ruled until 663 CE, waited for the monk with ministers, priests, incense and parasol. The king organized a feast where he threw the floor open for religious discussion. He fully sponsored the monk during his two-year stay in his kingdom and offered men to help him translate and transcribe scriptures. Most importantly, he introduced Xuanzang to the sage Sanghayasas and his entourage of nine monks.

The sage, a 70-year-old scholar, schooled his youthful disciple assiduously. Before noon, the pair tackled the *Abhidharmakosa*.

This work delineates the different schools of thought of early Buddhism and is a compendium intended to explain the words of the Buddha and the world according to the great master. In the present day, it has been preserved primarily in Tibetan and Chinese translations. Very little exists in Sanskrit.

In the afternoon, Xuanzang studied the *Nyayanusara Shastra*, a critique of the *Abhidharmakosa*. After the first watch of the night, the scholars turned to the Sanskrit education system. He was introduced to grammar and Indian logic, learnt to use valid arguments and perfected his elocution. He learnt the rules of debate, to speak in pure Sanskrit, and was taught not to show his nervousness or speak out of turn. His teacher was overjoyed with his pupil and proclaimed that Xuanzang was competent enough to join the line of the Yogachara teachers, the great Vasubandhu and Asanga.

Xuanzang gives a fascinating description of Kashmir. According to him, this place was once a lake where a Naga resided. Both the lake and the land were transferred to the Naga by Madhayantika, Ananda's disciple. The Naga wished to make religious offerings to Madhyantika, but Madhyantika was about to enter nirvana and could not grant his wish. The Naga then wished for 500 arhats to receive offerings from him. Thus, 50 years after the Buddha's nirvana, Madhyantika converted the Naga to Buddhism. He left the lake, founded 500 sangharamas, and invited sages and saints to live there.[22] Afterwards, in the four hundredth year of the Buddha's nirvana, Kanishka, the king of Gandhara, convened an assembly of scholars here. Five hundred of them came together, including the venerable monk Vasumitra, who led the assembly. First, they composed the *Upadesha Shastra* to explain the *Sutra Pitaka* of 10,000 stanzas, then the *Vinaya Vibasha Shastra* of equal length to explain the *Vinaya* and *Abhidharma*.

---

[22]Xuanzang, *Si-yu-ki: Buddhist Records of the Western World Book III*, Samuel Beal (trans.), Routledge, California, 2008, pp. 149–150.

The king ordered these shastras to be engraved on sheets of copper, which he enclosed in a stone chest. He then built a grand stupa and placed the chest within it.

Through Ancient India and the Hubs of Buddhism

From Kashmir, Xuanzang crossed the river Chandrabhaga (Chenab) to reach the town of Sakala, present-day Sialkot, in Pakistan. This was where Vasubandhu, the Indian monk and scholar who wrote a commentary on Abhidharma, lived for some time before moving to Ayodhya with his teachers Buddhamitra and Manoratha. Leaving this place, he arrived at a forest of palash trees and encountered a band of 50 robbers. They took all his clothes and belongings and pursued him and his companions, swords in hands, until they reached a dried-up marshland, ready to slay them all. Xuanzang and his companions saw a watercourse beyond, wide and deep enough to hide them. They rushed towards it, crossed it, and continued to run. Soon, they met a Brahmin ploughing his field. When they told him about the robbers, he was terrified but immediately gathered about 80 villagers, each of whom brought a weapon he could find. Together, they went to the robbers, who, seeing the crowd approaching, quickly withdrew and vanished into the forest. Xuanzang freed the men who were still bound while the villagers gave them some garments. While all of them were weeping and lamenting, Xuanzang was the only one smiling merrily. He told them that life was the greatest treasure. Now that their lives had been saved, they could always return what they had lost. His companions understood that Xuanzang was not easily perturbed, just as turbulent waves did not disturb the calm waters beneath. Xuanzang next went to Chinapati, in present-day Punjab, where he met the renowned priest Vinitaprabha, who had mastered the three Pitakas. Xuanzang stayed here for 14 months to study the *Abhidharma*, the *Nyaya Shastras*, and other tenets with him.

He then went to Jalandhara, where he met the eminent priest Chandravarna at the Nagaradhana convent. Chandravarna was thoroughly acquainted with the *Tripitaka*, so Xuanzang studied with him for four months. Traversing Kuluta, the present-day Kullu Valley, crossing a mountain range and a river, he came to the kingdom of Shatadru or Sutlej, and from there, he travelled to Mathura.

Mathura was an important Buddhist centre where he found stupas containing relics of the Buddha and his disciples, Sariputra, Maudgalyayana, Purnamaitrayaniputra, Upali, Ananda, Rahul and Manjushri. There were Buddhists who followed these masters according to their faith and beliefs. Xuanzang also found a mountain sangharama founded by Upagupta, where his relics, hair and nails lay.

He crossed the Yamuna and the Ganga and arrived at Matipura on the latter's banks in present-day Amroha. Here, he found the sangharama where Gunaprabha, a scholar of *Vinaya Pitaka* and a disciple of Vasubandhu, lived. A little to the south was the sangharama, where the renowned scholar Sanghabhadra spent the last years of his life. Originally a native of Kashmir, he was a man of distinguished knowledge. He thoroughly understood the vibhasha of the Sarvastivad school. By this time, Vasubandhu Bodhisattva had also distinguished himself for his learning. He had already composed the *Abhidharma Kosha-Shastra*, a text that was admired by all. After 12 years of reflection, Sanghabhadra composed the *Koshakarika Shastra*, consisting of 25,000 *shloka*s (verses) and 80,000 words, in which he refuted Vasubandhu. Having finished it, he longed to show it to Vasubandhu to settle the truth or falsehood of his points. However, he died without attaining his objective. Afterwards, Vasubandhu saw the treatise and praised it highly. He named it *Nyayanusara Shastra*.

After Sanghabhadra's death, a stupa was erected in his memory in a mango grove, which Xuanzang visited. Next to the grove was a stupa containing the relics of the scholar Vimalamitra, another native of Kashmir. As Vimalamitra passed by the stupa of Sanghabhadra, he was deeply saddened at the thought that his treatise had not been published before his death. He composed a treatise refuting the principles of Mahayana Buddhism and Vasubandhu while supporting Sanghabhadra. He felt this would immortalize the name of Sanghabhadra. However, he fell severely ill and thought that this was because he had refuted the principles of the great vehicle. He repented and destroyed his writing. He never recovered from the illness and breathed his last soon after.

Mitrasana, an eminent 90-year-old priest, also lived here. He was a disciple of Gunaprabha and a master of the *Tripitakas*. Xuanzang studied with him for a few months and then proceeded to travel through Brahmpura, Ahipura (Bareilly) and Kapitha. About 100 kilometres east of the city, he found a sangharama with ladders made of precious substances facing east and placed from south to north. It was believed that down one of these ladders, the Buddha descended from the Taryastrimshas, a heaven in Buddhist cosmology where 33 gods reside. He had gone to preach for the sake of his queen mother, Maya, and then returned to Jambudvipa. The middle ladder was made of gold, on the left was a crystal ladder, and on the right it was made of silver. It was believed that the Buddha descended from the middle ladder accompanied by 100,000 devas and great bodhisattvas. The precious stone ladders had disappeared, and subsequent kings reconstructed them from stone and brick and ornamented them with various gems, raising them to about 70 feet.

Xuanzang next went to Kannauj, the kingdom of the renowned king Harshavardhana, whose elder brother Rajyavardhana had been murdered by the rival king of Bengal, Shashanka. Then, the minister Bhani, or Bhandi, installed Shiladitya Harshavardhana (Xuanzang refers to him in his writings) on the throne. Harshavardhana combined military talents with a strong sense of justice. He soon avenged his brother and made himself the ruler of India, which, in effect, was the present-day northern India. Under Harshavardhana's rule, peace prevailed—the king did a lot of charity and encouraged scholarship in his kingdom. When Xuanzang entered this kingdom, he went to the temple called Bhadravihara. There, he stopped for three months and read the *vibhasa* (compendium) of Buddhadasa called *Varmavibhasa Vyakarana*, under the direction of Viryasena, a master of the *Tripitaka*. Xuanzang subsequently went to Ayodhya, where he found about a 100 temples and thousands of priests studying Hinayana and Mahayana Buddhism. He saw the sangharama where Bodhisattva Vasubandhu composed his treatise on the Hinayana and Mahayana. A little distance away was a stupa built by Ashoka on the spot where the Buddha had preached for three months. Nearby was also the sangharama, where Bodhisattva Asanga taught. Having paid his respects to all these holy sites, Xuanzang set off for Hayamukh, a place between Ayodhya and Prayag along the course of the Ganga.

After travelling some 50 kilometres, he was waylaid by pirates. Both riverbanks were covered with thick ashoka forests in which pirate boats were hidden. These pirates were devotees of Goddess Durga, and it was the season of sacrifice. Seeing the perfect form of Xuanzang, they decided that he was appropriate for the human sacrifice they had planned. Xuanzang humbly said that he was ready, but he had travelled all the way to India to offer his reverence to the image of Bodhi and the Gridhrakuta Mountain and to learn the sacred books. Since his purpose had not yet been accomplished, he said, if the pirates killed him, they would only bring misfortune upon themselves. His fellow passengers also pleaded with the pirates to spare him.

The captain was impervious to their pleas and dispatched men to fetch water, prepare the ground for the sacrifice, and erect an altar. He commanded two others to sharpen their knives and bind Xuanzang to the altar. Even when they were about to behead him, Xuanzang showed no fear, which greatly astonished the pirates. His only request to the pirates was not to crowd around him; he wanted to depart with a joyous mind. Before his impending death, he prayed that he may return to earth to convert these men and the rest of the world to virtue. He was deep in meditation while his fellow passengers were shouting and crying. Suddenly, a huge tempest arose. Sand flew in all directions and the boats rocked violently. The pirates took this as an omen, a punishment for what they were about to do. They asked who he was, and when they learnt he was a great holy man from China, they fell at his feet. They gave up robbery and converted to Buddhism.

After passing through Hayamukh, Xuanzang reached Prayag, where he defeated the Brahmins in debate and saw the stupa which marked the place where the Buddha overcame the heretics. He also saw the Field of Great Beneficence, where, from ancient times, kings had given away wealth in charity. The Field of Great Beneficence was a plain to the west of the confluence of the Ganga and the Yamuna, where the king set up a great convocation every five years to which all the shramanas and Brahmins were invited. To gain religious merit, the king distributed all the wealth he possessed to them and the needy until the entire treasury was exhausted, barring that which was required to maintain law and order and govern the kingdom. Shiladitya Harshavardhana also followed this practice and gave away the accumulated wealth of five years within a span of 75 days.

From Prayag, Xuanzang went to Kaushambi, where he found a sangharama with a sandalwood figure of the Buddha. Legend has it that in old times, Tathagata or Buddha dwelt in the heavens for three months during the resting period or *vassato* to preach to his mother. The king, Udayan, who was ruling at that time, thinking of him with affection, requested Maudgalyayana to transport a clever sculptor to heaven to observe the Buddha's form and features so that he could carve a sandalwood statue of the Buddha on his return. When the Buddha descended from the heavens, the figure of sandalwood rose to greet him.[23]

A short distance from Kaushambi was a double-storeyed tower where Vasubandhu composed the *Vidyamatra-siddhi Shastra*. A little further was a mango grove in which some old foundation stones were present. It was here that Asanga Bodhisattva composed the *Prakararanaryavacha-Shastra-Karika*. About 250 kilometres from here was Vishakha, where there were two sangharamas with about 3,000 priests who followed the Hinayana. Some distance away was another sangharama where the arhat Devasharman composed the *Vigyana-Kaya-Beda-Shastra* in the olden days, which affirms the non-existence of the 'self' or the individual. Here, the arhat Gopa also composed a *shastra* affirming the exact opposite: the existence of the 'self' or the individual. These two works led to many treatises affirming one or the other. This was also where Dharmapada Boddhisattva overthrew a 100 writers of the shastra belonging to the Hinayana. Beside this spot was where the Tathagata preached Dhamma for six years.

Going northeast for about 250 kilometres, Xuanzang arrived at the kingdom of Shravasti, where there were hundreds of sangharamas with thousands of priests, all following Hinayana Buddhism. King Prasanjita dwelt in the capital of this kingdom at the time of the Buddha. Within the city, Xuanzang found old ruins of the king's palace and a stupa erected on old foundations. Prasanjita had also erected a preaching hall for the Buddha here. There was also a tower where the vihara of Prajapati Bhikkhuni, the Buddha's older maternal aunt, stood. Nearby was another tower that marked the ruined house of Sudatta, a wealthy merchant from Buddha's time who was his chief patron. By its side was a great stupa at the spot where Angulimal, the ruthless brigand, had given up his evil designs after converting to Buddhism.

---

[23]Xuanzang, *Si-yu-ki: Buddhist Records of the Western World Book V*, Samuel Beal (trans.), Routledge, California, 2008, pp. 235–236.

There were also multiple bottomless chasms, which were believed to be places where those who slandered the Buddha, like Devadatta, sank and went to hell.[24]

From there, Xuanzang went to Kapilavastu. While the place was wasted and ruined, he found a few old foundations of the chief palace of King Suddhodana over which a vihara had been built. Inside was the statue of the king. To the north of it were the ruins of Queen Maya's sleeping hall. A vihara had also been built over this and the queen's statue was placed in it. Beside this vihara was where the Shakya Bodhisattva is said to have descended as a spirit into his mother's womb. To the northeast, Xuanzang found a stupa marking the spot where Rishi Asita had seen the prince's horoscope. He also saw the field where the prince played sports with his companions. Another place marked the spot where Prince Siddhartha left his palace on horseback to search for the truth. Other places marked the spots where the prince saw the old man, the sick man, the dead man and the shaman, who had given up the world. This made Gautam Buddha return to his palace in deep thought.

Xuanzang went about 50 kilometres eastward and reached a forest where King Ashoka had built a great stupa at the spot where Gautam Buddha had cut off his hair, removed his ornaments and rich garb, and tiara, and given it all to Chandaka, who had been the servant and charioteer of Prince Siddhartha.

Leaving the forest, Xuanzang came to Kushinagara, which was utterly desolate. Within the city was a stupa built by King Ashoka on the site of the old house of Chunda, the blacksmith who had given the Buddha his last meal which resulted in him contracting fatal dysentery. Two to three kilometres to the northwest, he crossed the river Ajitavati and came to a Shala grove, the place where the Buddha breathed his last. Here, he found a great vihara built of bricks within which was a figure

---

[24]Ibid., 2–9.

of the nirvana of Tathagata. Next to it stood a huge stupa built by King Ashoka.

After another 250 kilometres or so, passing through a great forest, Xuanzang came to the city of Banaras, where he saw the place where the Buddha preached his first sermon. From here, he travelled to Vaishali. While the place was in ruins, a stupa marked the site where the Buddha recited the *Vimalakirtti Sutra*. Some distance from there, Xuanzang found the ruins of Vimalakirtti's house, from which many strange spiritual portents or signs were said to arise.[25] A little to the north was where Vimalakirtti preached, and a stupa marked the spot where the Buddha stopped on his way to Kushinagara to attain nirvana. Here, he saw where Ambapali gave the garden to the Buddha.

Leaving Vaishali, travelling through Svetapura, and crossing the Ganga, Xuanzang reached Magadha. Here, he found about 50 sangharamas with 10,000 priests, mostly Mahayana followers. About 35 kilometres south, he came to an old, desolate town. It was once called Kusumapura, a name derived from the king's palace, which had a great abundance of flowers. Later, it came to be known as Pataliputra. A hundred years after the Buddha's nirvana, King Ashoka, the great-grandson of King Bimbisara, transferred his court from Rajagriha to Pataliputra. However, when Xuanzang arrived here, only ruins remained.

Arrival in Nalanda

After travelling to and paying his respects at all the places associated with the Buddha, Xuanzang reached Nalanda. The monks there had already heard of his arrival and selected four distinguished scholars to meet him. Journeying in their company, he reached the farmhouse belonging to Nalanda, where Maudgalyayana

---

[25]Xuanzang, *Si-yu-ki: Buddhist Records of the Western World Book VI*, Samuel Beal (trans.), Routledge, California, 2008, pp. 66–68.

was born. Making a brief halt for refreshments, Xuanzang entered Nalanda accompanied by 200 priests and 1,000 laymen. Here, he was joined by the whole body of the community, which placed a special seat for him by the side of the *sthavira* or the presiding priest. It was announced that the institution would look after all his needs and that he would enjoy all the applications of the religion. Twenty middle-aged men—dignified scholars—were deputed to conduct him in the presence of the head of Nalanda, the venerable Shilabhadra.

After exchanging courtesies, Xuanzang expressed his desire to learn the principles of Yogachara from Shilabhadra. Hearing this, Shilabhadra called his disciple Buddhabhadra with tears in his eyes. Buddhabhadra was Shilabhadra's nephew, himself over 70 years old, thoroughly versed in the sutras and shastras, and had an excellent ability to discourse. Shilabhadra asked Buddhabhadra to recount the former's ill-health and suffering over the past three years. He had been suffering from severe joint pain for 20 years and had become wholly incapacitated in the last three years. So severe was his suffering that he hated his life and wished to die. However, one night, he dreamt that three devas appeared in shining garments, one the colour of gold, the second of crystal, and the last of silver. They asked him if he was anxious to get rid of his body and exhorted that he was suffering because, in his past life, he was a king who had caused much suffering to all living creatures. They urged him to introspect, find his past faults, and sincerely repent them. They told Shilabhadra to bear his affliction quietly and patiently, and to preach the sutras and shastras diligently if he wanted to get rid of his pain. However, if he continued to loathe his body, there would be no cessation of his suffering. These three figures were Avalokiteshvara Boddhisattva, Maitreya Boddhisattva and Manjushri Boddhisattva. They foretold that a priest from China would visit, desirous of studying with him, and that he must instruct him carefully. Having said this, they disappeared, as did Shilabhadra's suffering.

On hearing this, Xuanzang was emotionally overwhelmed and paid his respects to him. By now, Xuanzang had been travelling for three years. He vowed to listen to and practise his religious advice with all his strength if the great Shilabhadra showed compassion and accepted him as his student. After this, Xuanzang retired and went to King Baladitya's college. There, he took up residence with Balabhadra, who looked after him for seven days. He was then sent to the dwelling of Dharmapala Bodhisattva, where he was provided with everything he needed.

Xuanzang visited all the places in the vicinity that had been made sacred by the Buddha and then returned to Nalanda, requesting Shilabhadra to explain the *Yoga Shastra* to him. He had already studied the *Kosha Shastra*, the *Vibhasha Shastra*, and the *Shatpadabhidharma Shastra* in Kashmir, but he studied them again to remove some doubts. After this, he devoted himself to studying Hindu texts and *vyakarana* (or *vyakaranam*), grammar, and 'a treatise relating to the record of the science of sounds'. In the five years of study, Xuanzang mastered all Buddhist and Hindu sacred book collections.

The Return Journey

Xuanzang's return journey was as tricky and adventurous as his journey to India. He finally reached Khotan, where he sent a young man of Kau-Chang with a letter to the emperor, informing him of his return and requesting help transporting the books he had brought from India. China, he said, had always held its ancient scholars and masters of public morals in high esteem. Hence, those who went to research the source of the teachings of Buddha and brought them back to China should be equally admired:

> [...] (I)f we admire these ancient masters, for thus going afar in search (or, *support of*) learning, how much more those who search into the secret traces of the profit-bringing

religion of the Buddhas, and the marvellous words of the three Pit.akas, able to liberate from the snares of the world? How can we dare to undervalue such labours, or not regard them with ardour? Now I, Hiuen-Tsiang, long since versed in the doctrine of the Buddha, bequeathed by him in the Western world, the rules and precepts of which had reached the East in an imperfect form, always pondered on a plan for searching out the true learning, without any thought for personal safety. Accordingly, in the fourth month of the third year of the period Chêng-Kwan (630, AD), braving dangers and obstacles, I secretly found my way to India. I travelled over vast plains of shifting sand: I scaled precipitous mountain crags clad with snow: found my way through scarped passes of the iron' gates; passed along by the tumultuous waves of the hot sea. Beginning at the sacred city of Chang'an, I reached the new city of Râjagr. iha.

Thus, I accomplished a journey of more than 50,000 *li*; yet notwithstanding the thousand differences of customs and manners I have witnessed, the myriads of dangers I have encountered, by the goodness of heaven, I have returned without accident, and now offer my homage with the body unimpaired, and I am satisfied with the accomplishment of my vows. I have beheld the great Ghṛidhrakûṭa Mountain, worshipped at the Bôdhi tree; I have seen traces not seen before; heard sacred words not heard before; witnessed spiritual prodigies, exceeding all the wonders of nature; have borne testimony to the high qualities of our august Emperor; and won for him the highest team and praise of the people. In my travels through successive kingdoms, I have passed seventeen years, and now, having come from the country of Prayâga; passed through Kapiśa, surmounted the precipices of T'sung-Ling, traversed the valley of Pamir, I have reached Khotan.

And now, because the great elephant (*which I had*) perished in the waters, I have not yet succeeded in obtaining transport for the numerous books, which I have brought back. On that account, I have remained here a little while; but not having obtained (*even here*) the necessary mode of conveyance, I purpose at once to go forward and visit your Majesty. With this view, I have sent forward a layman belonging to Kau-Chang, whose name is *Ma-huan-chi*, in the company of certain merchants, respectfully to present this letter and to announce my purpose.[26]

He then propounded the principles of the *Yoga Shastra*, the *Abhidharma Shastra*, the *Kosha Shastra* and the *Mahayana Samparigraha Shastra* to the priests of Khotan by day and night. The king and lay people also attended his teachings, and many thousands embraced the faith daily.

After seven or eight months, the messenger returned with a gracious message from the king to this effect:

When I heard that the master who had gone to far-off countries to search for religious books, had now come back, I was filled with joy without bounds. I pray you come quickly, that we may see each other. The priests of this kingdom, who understand the *Fan* language and the explanation of the sacred books, I have also commanded to come and pay you a greeting. I have ordered the bureaux of Khotan and other places to send with you the best guides they can procure and conveyances as many as you require. I have commanded the magistrates of Tun-wang to conduct you through the desert of shifting sands, and I have desired the Shen-Shen (*government*) to send to meet you at Tso moh.[27]

---

[26]Li, Hwui, *The Life of Hiuen-tsiang*, Samuel Beal (trans.), Kegan Paul Trench Trubner and Company Limited, London, 1914, pp. 209–210.
[27]Ibid., 210.

On receiving this letter, Xuanzang immediately proceeded to China. The king of Khotan provided him with an ample supply of provisions, and after another long journey, Xuanzang arrived at his country's borders. He sent back the messengers from Khotan who had accompanied him to this point. They returned, declining any recompense for their services.

Having reached Sha-Chow, Xuanzang wrote another letter to the emperor, who was in Loyang then. When the emperor learnt that Xuanzang was gradually approaching, he commanded Fong-Huang-ling, duke of the kingdom of Liang and the governor of the western capital, to receive Xuanzang with all proper ceremonies. Xuanzang knew the emperor would want to question why he had left the country without permission. Wishing to avoid giving the impression of any delay, he pressed forward with haste and took a shorter route via a canal.[28]

The magistrates did not know the polite reception and escort protocol and could not make the necessary preparations. However, news of Xuanzang's arrival spread fast, and people came in large numbers of their own accord to see him and pay their respects. The streets were so crowded that Xuanzang could not disembark, so he spent the night on the canal. The following day, he was escorted to the western capital of Si-gan-fu, where he arrived in the spring of 645 CE. The next day, the members of the various ministries took him, with flags and banners, to the convent called Hong-fu. Here, he deposited the treasures he had brought from India—relics of the Buddha and several of his many-foot-tall statues, made of gold, sandalwood, silver, and translucent material, all signifying different events and miracles associated with the Buddha's life.

He also deposited in this temple the Mahayana books he had brought with him, which included 224 sutras, 192 shastras, and 15 works of the Sthavira school, including sutras, vinayas and shastras; the exact number belongs to the Sammatiya school;

---

[28]Ibid., 212.

22 similar works of the Mahishasaka school; 67 books of the Sarvastivada school; 17 of the Kashyapi school; 42 works of the Dharmagupta school; 36 copies of the *Hetuvidya Shastra*; 13 copies of the *Shabdavidya Shastra*; a total of 520 fascicles, comprising 657 distinct volumes, carried upon 20 horses.

After visiting the chief officers of the western capital, Xuanzang proceeded to Loyang to meet the emperor. While he received the greatest attention at the I-lawn Palace, Emperor Taizong asked him why he had left China without consulting him. Xuanzang replied that he had sent three requests for permission to leave the country before his departure. However, he did not receive any answers, and being unable to restrain his desire to go to India in search of Buddhist texts, he left without permission.

After a long conversation during which Xuanzang declined the offer of a secular life, he retired to the Hong-fu Temple in Si-gan-fu to begin his translation work. For this purpose, he requested Emperor Taizong to set up a board of 12 experts in Buddhist literature from monasteries all over China, nine 'phrase connectors' to ensure the syntactical construction of the sentences was intelligible, and an expert in Sanskrit. Among the phrase connectors were Hui Li and Tao-hsuan, both biographers of Xuanzang, and the great lexicographer Tao-ying. The Sanskrit expert was Hsuan-mo, who had helped Prabhakaramitra with his translation work 15 years earlier.

By the end of 648 CE, Xuanzang had completed 58 books, including the *Si-Yu-Ki*—the records or history of the Western world—undertaken at the express command of Emperor Taizong. That year, the emperor, who was in bad health, went to his summer palace, the Jade Flower Palace—also called the Jade Flower Monastery—about 80 kilometres from Chang'an, and asked Xuanzang to join him, offering him a high official position again, as he had done in 645 CE. When he realized Xuanzang was sincere in his refusal, he promised to help him in his path.

He also agreed to write the preface to Xuanzang's work. In October 648 CE, Emperor Taizong returned to Chang'an and asked Xuanzang to live with him in the palace. This made it difficult for Xuanzang to work uninterruptedly, as the emperor wanted to speak to him and ask him to explain Buddhist precepts. The crown prince at this time announced that the monastery he had built in memory of his mother, who had died at the young age of 35, was complete. It was to be called TaT'zu-en Sen, or the Great Monastery of Maternal Love. It was beside the Serpentine Lake, and one of its ten courtyards was set up for Xuanzang and his team of translators. At the end of the year, the books and paintings that Xuanzang had brought from India were moved from the Hong-fu Temple to the Monastery of Maternal Love.

Emperor Taizong died in 650 CE and was succeeded by Kaotsung. Xuanzang now devoted himself earnestly to his translation work. He rose every morning at dawn and after a slight repast, devoted four hours to explaining the sacred books. Apart from looking after the monastery, he delivered lectures attended by more than a hundred people, including his 100 disciples, princes and ministers. He discoursed mainly on the various systems of the schools and the distinguished Buddhist masters and teachers from India. In 652 CE, Xuanzang requested the king to construct a pagoda at the southern gate of the Hong-fu Temple, where he eventually deposited his sacred books and images for safety. This came to be known as the Wild Goose Pagoda. The total height of the structure was 180 feet. It was modelled on Indian stupas and had five stages, surmounted by a cupola. On the highest storey on the southern side was a chamber in which copies of the two prefaces composed by the former emperor and the princes were preserved, in addition to the volumes translated by Xuanzang. The prefaces were in the handwriting of Ch'u Sul-Liang, the most well-known calligrapher of the time.

In 654 CE, Dharmarudha, a monk from the Mahabodhi

Temple in Central India, met Xuanzang. He brought with him
a letter which said:

> The Venerable Prajñādeva, who is surrounded by a group
> of well-learned scholars of the Mahābodhi Monastery at
> the Vajrāsana of the Buddha, The Abstruse and Auspicious
> One, sends his best greetings to the Mokṣācārya of Mahā-
> Cina who is erudite in the sublime teachings of the Tripiṭ
> aka and wishes him in his best health.
>
> I, Bhikṣu Prajñādeva, have composed a stanza in praise
> of the great divine powers of the Buddha, as well as the
> sutras, śāstras and the Four Noble Truths, which I have
> entrusted Bhikṣu Dharmarudha to send to you.
>
> The old virtuous Ācārya Jñānaprabha of this place whose
> knowledge is unlimited, also sends his greetings to you, and
> Upāsaka Sūryalabdha also pays his homage to you.
>
> We are now sending you two rolls of white cotton cloth
> to show our remembrance of you. As the way is too far, we
> hope that you will accept it without thinking it is too small
> a gift. If you are in need of any sūtra or śāstra, you may
> just give us a list and we shall make copies of the required
> books for your use.[29]

Xuanzang acknowledged the honour conferred upon him.
Dharmarudha stayed in China for two years and returned with
Xuanzang's letters for Jnanaprabha and Prajnadeva. In his letter to
Jnanaprabha, he said that Chinese envoys had gone to India, from
where they returned in 648 CE with the sad news of the passing
of Shilabhadra, his teacher at Nalanda. He continued:

> The boat on the sea of suffering has sunk, and the eyes of
> devas and men have closed. His death is all too soon for

---

[29]Li, Hwui, *The Life of Hsuan Tsang*, Li Yung-Hsi (trans.), Samyak Prakashan, New Delhi, 2023, p. 235.

us. The Right Dharma-Keeper had cultivated good deeds
and performed meritorious acts during a long period in
his past lives...

Now that the teacher is dead, it is your turn to succeed
to his post. I hope your eloquence in preaching will always
be as fluent as water in the four seas, and your adornments
of felicity and wisdom will be as permanent as the five
mountains.[30]

He said that since his return, he had translated the *Yoga Shastra*
and about 30 other works, great and small. He had still not
finished the *Kosha* and the *Nyayanusara* but hoped to do so by
the end of the year. He also sent some small gifts and requested
the replacement of the books he had lost while crossing the river
Indus on his way back to China.

The letter to Prajnadeva is intriguing. There was rivalry
between the two, and despite the lapse of time and the gracious
gesture of Prajnadeva, Xuanzang still invokes it. He says:

Being a man of ordinary ability, I am growing weak, and
my remembrance of your virtues and my admiration for
your benignity make me think of you all the more. When
I was studying in India, I had the opportunity to meet
your Reverance, and in the meeting of Kanyākubja, we had
debated together to find out the truth in the presence of
kings and numerous followers of different schools. It was
unavoidable that there had been bitter arguments as one
party holding the doctrines of Mahāyānism, while the other
party the teachings of Hinayānism. Truth was what was
sought after, regardless of personal feelings. Thus, I had
probably offended you during the course of debate, but as
soon as the meeting was over, all resentment was cleared
immediately. Now the messenger still again conveyed to me

---

[30]Ibid., 236–238.

your apology for that event. How scrupulous you are! You are a good scholar of great eloquence and noble character.[31]

However, despite the lapse of years, Xuanzang could not resist championing Mahayanism. He says:

> Being a man of virtue, you are an example to your students, and I hope that you will exert yourself to spread the right Dharma. No doctrine is as perfect as Mahāyāna Buddhism, and I regret that you did not have a deep faith in it. It is like those who are content with a sheep or deer cart but give up a bull carriage. One should appreciate crystal instead of a piece of glass.[32]

During the years 655 CE and 656 CE, while Xuanzang continued to translate his books, a new heir apparent was installed. He celebrated his position by giving a banquet attended by 5,000 monks at the Monastery of Maternal Love. During its course, two officials visited Xuanzang and asked him if he needed help. He requested that the emperor allow an imperial inscription to be put up at the monastery describing the circumstances of its creation. To this, the emperor agreed and an inscription in running hand was finally put up. At the end, the emperor wrote 'Hsien ch'ing First Year' in his calligraphic style.

The Final Journey

A few weeks later, Xuanzang fell ill with a disease he had contracted while crossing the mountains of India. He partially recovered with the help of the physicians sent from the court. The emperor invited Xuanzang to stay with him in Loyang for a while as that would provide him with a much-needed change.

---

[31]Ibid., 239.
[32]Ibid., 239–240.

He was given a place in the Ying-ying Hall of the palace but later returned to the Monastery of Maternal Love. On the way, he went to his birthplace, about 20 kilometres from Loyang, as his parents had not been given a proper funeral. His older brother was already dead, so Xuanzang had his parents re-interred. He wanted to retire to a small rural monastery there, the Small Forest Monastery, and wrote to the emperor to seek his permission, which was, of course, emphatically denied.

Xuanzang was now anxious that he might not finish the translation of the *Prajnaparamita* with his advancing age and failing health. He wanted to work undisturbed, so he was permitted to go to the isolated Jade Flower Monastery (Palace). He moved into the palace in 659 CE and began the translation in 660 CE. The Indian copy of the *Mahaprajnaparamita Sutra* consisted of 200,000 shlokas; he proposed to produce an abridged translation but was warned in a dream not to do so. Xuanzang had procured three copies of this work in India, which he collated to form the correct text he would translate. He was now 65 years old and had a feeling that his end was near. He worked without interruption to finish his task before his death and completed it at the end of 663 CE. His entire work of the *Mahaprajnaparamita Sutra* consists of 600 chapters in 12 volumes.

He then prepared for his funeral, telling his disciples to bury him wrapped in an ordinary mat on the banks of a mountain stream far from the monastery. When his disciples said that he looked well enough, he replied that while he might appear so, he knew his time had come.

On New Year's Day of 664 CE, the disciples asked Xuanzang what work he would undertake next and whether he would translate the *Ratna-kut Sutra*, another voluminous work. He declined and said,

> This sūtra is as voluminous as the *Mahāprajñā-pāramitā Sūtra*. Considering my energy, I know that I am unable to

complete this work. I am not far from the time of my death. Now, I intend to visit the Lanchih Valley and the other places to pay my last homage to the ten koṭi Buddha's images.[33]

He must have installed them there at some point in time. He set off with his disciples, and they watched with tears in their eyes as he performed his devotions. On his return to the monastery, he gave himself entirely to religious exercises and no longer translated. A monk had a strange dream and went to Xuanzang. He dreamt of a high and beautiful pagoda which suddenly teetered and fell. Xuanzang told him that the dream had nothing to do with the monk but portended Xuanzang's death.

The following day, Xuanzang tripped over a brick culvert and grazed his leg. At first, he felt all right, but four or five days later, he was so unwell that he lay on the bed with his eyes open. Again and again, he saw a large white lotus flower. On the seventeenth day, he saw hundreds and thousands of tall men dressed in silk. They decorated his room and the monastery with embroideries, beautiful flowers and valuable jewels.[34] They also lined up all kinds of delicious dishes unknown in this world, but Xuanzang refused to eat any of it, as he felt that such food was meant for arhats and he was far below them. This was all, of course, a figment of his imagination. Just then, he regained consciousness because one of the monks at his bedside happened to cough. Xuanzang narrated all this to the abbot of the monastery, adding that all that was brought to him symbolized his work.

He then asked one of his disciples, Chia-Shang, to make a list of all the books he had translated, paintings he had made, texts he had reproduced, the many thousands of poor people he had supported, teachers he had brought honour to, lamps he had lit, and living creatures he had ransomed from death. When the

---

[33]Ibid., 265.
[34]Ibid., 266.

list was made, he asked Chia-Shang to read it aloud. At the end of the recital, he closed his eyes and lay perfectly still. On the twenty-third day, he prepared a feast for the monks and offered them alms. He asked Sung Fa-chih, a sculptor, to make a full-scale clay sculpture of the Buddha in the posture of enlightenment, sitting under the Bodhi Tree, the image of which the envoy Wang Hiuen-Tse had brought back from India.[35] It was to be installed in the Buddha Hall of the monastery. He said farewell to his fellow translators and disciples:

> This physical body of mine is loathsome. Since my work has been accomplished, it is unnecessary for me to stay any longer. I wish to offer all the merits of my good deeds to all living beings so that we may all be reborn to the Tus. ita Heaven to serve Maitreya Bodhisattva, and when the future Buddha comes down to the human world, we may also descend with him to perform Buddhist tasks until we attain supreme enlightenment![36]

As per legend, Tushita Heaven is where the future Buddha, Maitreya, awaits his time for coming to Earth.

He stayed in silent meditation for a while and then was heard murmuring,

> Form is unreal. Perception, thought, action, knowledge— all are unreal. The eye, the ear, the mind—all are unreal. Consciousness through the Five Senses is unreal. All the Twelve Causes, from ignorance to Old Age and Death, are unreal. Enlightenment is unreal. Unreality itself is unreal.

Then he made those around him recite: 'Homage to Maitreya Tathagata, the Fully Enlightened One! May I be reborn among

---

[35]Ibid., 265–266.
[36]Ibid., 267–268.

them after I have forsaken my present life!'[37]

Gradually, his breathing became fainter and fainter, and he kept sinking slowly until the day of his death, on the thirteenth day of the tenth month of the year 664 CE. He was buried in the western capital, but in the year 669 CE, his remains were removed by order of the emperor to a space situated north of the Valley of Fan-chuen, where a tower was constructed in his memory.

---

[37]Ibid., 268.

4

Nalanda: The Venerable Seat of Learning

Early History

Fa-hien, who toured India in the early years of the fifth century CE, does not mention Nalanda. All he says is that one yojana, southwest of a particular place, brought them to the village of Nala, where Sariputra, one of the primary disciples of the Buddha, was born and where he returned to attain his parinirvana. At the spot, a stupa was built which still exists today. Nala, according to Fa-hien, was one yojana from Giryek or the old Rajagriha and the same distance from the new Rajagriha; Nalanda too was one yojana from Rajagriha, and thus, Nala was identified with Nalanda. According to the *Maha Sudassana Jataka*, another ancient Pali text, Sariputra was not born in Nala but in an unimportant village, Nalagram, as the Jataka expressly calls it, which was also known as Nalaka. Probably, Fa-hien did not visit Nalanda, so he did not give a proper account of the place. However, it is difficult to understand why he did not go to Nalanda in Magadha, an important place associated with Gautam Buddha and Tirthankara Mahavira.

From Nala to Nalanda

The confusion over Nalanda remained until as late as 1500 CE. Taranath (157–163 CE), a Tibetan Lama of the Jonang School of

Tibetan Buddhism, wrote the history of Buddhism and is a good source of information on what followed in the centuries after the death of the Buddha. He observes Nalanda was, in former times,

> [...] (T)he birthplace of the Śāriputra, was also the place where he, with eighty thousand *arhat-s*, attained nirvāṇa. In the meanwhile, the *brāhmaṇa* settlement fell into ruins. Only the *caitya* of the venerable Śāriputra remained. King Aśoka elaborately worshipped it and built a large temple of the Buddha there...
> Thus, Aśoka was the founder of the first vihara at *Nalendra.[38]

Taranath also mentions a tradition according to which Nagarjuna and Aryadeva, in around 100 CE, were the forerunners among those who took an interest in the educational institutions of the place. To mention another tradition written about by Taranath, Suvishnu, a contemporary of Nagarjuna, is said to have established 108 temples at Nalanda to prevent any decline of *Abhidhamma*, the ancient Buddhist texts, dated third century BCE and later, which contain detailed scholastic reworkings of the doctrinal material appearing in the Buddhist sutras, according to schematic classifications.

Xuanzang and I-Ching make no mistake in giving the correct name of the place. Xuanzang, at the beginning of his account of Nalanda, discusses theories on the origin of the name. He says:

> Going north from this (Patliputra or modern Patna, Xuanzang's location at the time) 30 li or so, we come to Nâlanda *sanghârâmas*. The old accounts of the country say that to the south of this *sanghârâmas*, in the middle of an Âmra ('An-mo-lo) [mango] grove, there is a tank. The Nâga

---

[38]Taranatha, *History of Buddhism in India*, Lama Chimpa and Alaka Chattodpadhaya (trans.), Delhi, Motilal Banarsidass Publishers, 2018, p. 101.

of this tank was called Nâlanda. By the side of it is built the *sanghârâmas*, which therefore takes the name (*of the Nâga*).[39]

In another account of the place, which Xuanzang thinks is correct, he says:

> But the truth is that Tathâgata in the old days practiced the life of a Bôdhisattva here and became the king of a great country and established his capital in the land. Moved by pity for living things, he delighted in continually relieving them. In remembrance of this virtue, he was styled charity without intermission, and the sangharama was called the perpetuation of his name.[40]

I-Ching, who visited India after Xuanzang, believed that Nalanda derived its name from the Naga Nanda, whom Xuanzang called Nalanda. It could be that Xuanzang also used Nalanda as a short form for Naga Nanda. Whatever the reason for Fa-hien's sketchy description, the fact is that there was a mango grove, a tank and perhaps also the Naga. As the Buddha walked through the country, he usually stayed in a grove. As for the tank, General Cunningham, who examined the place and conducted excavations there in the latter part of the nineteenth century, said, 'There still exists immediately to the south of the ruined monastery, a small tank called Kargidya Pokhar, that exactly answers to the position of the Nalanda tank...'[41]

Dharmasvamin, a Tibetan monk who visited the place much later, almost at the time of the decline, in 1234 CE, gives the name Nalanda, which in the Tibetan language means 'lord of men', and

---

[39]Xuanzang, *Si-yu-ki: Buddhist Records of the Western World*, Book IX, Samuel Beal (trans.), Routledge, California, 2008, p. 167.

[40]Ibid., 167.

[41]Cunningham, Alexander, *The Ancient Geography of India*, Gyan Publishing House, Delhi, 2006, pp. 306–307.

adds that a former raja built it and thus was given this name.[42] Hirananda Sastri, a reputed Indian archaeologist and an official of the Archaeological Survey of India, thought that the name was derived from *nala* (lotus stalks) because Nalanda has many lotus ponds. Thus, it would mean 'the giver of lotus stalks'.[43]

The Historical Auspiciousness of Nalanda

The early history of the place, as described in Buddhist texts, shows that Nalanda was a rich and prosperous city. To take just one illustration from the *Sutrakritanga Sutra*, the well-known Jain text, it is said that Lepa, one of the inhabitants of Nalanda, was prosperous, famous and rich. Abound in riches, gold and silver, he had large houses, beds, seats, vehicles and chariots, possessed many valuable and necessary things, owned many male and female slaves, and had stables full of cows, buffaloes and sheep. Even the great Buddha had partaken of Lepa's hospitality. Lepa offered his rich bathing halls to the enlightened Shakya prince, who gladly accepted them and delivered a long discourse that converted Udaka, who came to meet him, to Buddhism. The *Sutrakritanga Sutra* also describes Nalanda as a prosperous place with hundreds of buildings. Nalanda not only carried the legacy of the Buddha but also that of Lord Mahavira, the twenty-third Jain Tirthankara. It was the place where the great Mahavira met Gosala, who became his disciple and travelled with him for six years.

Nalanda was thus already imbued with the holy memories of the Buddha and Tirthankara Mahavira. Nalanda had a unique position among the many places where the Buddha preached.

---

[42]*Biography of Dharmaswamin: A Tibetan Monk Pilgrim*, Dr George Roerich (trans.), published on behalf of Kashi Prasad Jayaswal Research Institute, Patna, 1959, p. 90.

[43]Sastri, Hirananda, 'Nalanda and its Epigraphic Material', *Memoirs of the Archaeological Survey of India*, Issue No. 66, Calcutta, 1942, pp. 3–4.

He often visited with his favourite disciple, Ananda, and stayed at the Pavarika mango grove. When the Buddha chose Kushinagara as the place of his nirvana, Ananda thought that Nalanda was the most befitting for it.

The great temple built by Ashoka and other smaller ones by Brahmin Suvishnu, along with the fact that the Buddha had spent many happy days in Nalanda in the past, must have attracted King Kumaragupta to this place. He would go on to build the historic city of Nalanda, which would eventually become a prominent seat of learning.

A Prophetic Beginning and the Rise of the Great Seat of Learning

There are several reasons Nalanda, among all places in Magadha, became an epicentre of higher learning. Xuanzang enumerates how the sangharamas at Nalanda underwent different stages to gradually evolve into a residential university and not just remain a mere shelter for bhikkus to resort to for religious purposes.

In this context, the story of the prophecy made to the Gupta king Kumaragupta I—also referred to as Shakraditya— is interesting. It is said that when King Shakraditya selected a lucky spot and an auspicious moment to start digging to lay the foundation of the sangharama, Naga Nanda was accidentally wounded. This was an ill omen as Nagas were held sacred. The king consulted a soothsayer to confirm whether to proceed with the work. The soothsayer assured him that this was a superior site—if the king chose to build a sangharama here, it would become highly renowned and be a model for a thousand years as it continued to flourish. Students from all over would come here for their education. But at the same time, he warned, many would spill blood because of the wound inflicted on the Naga. Some truth to this prophecy can be seen in the various ups and downs in the life of Nalanda, which flourished, if not for a thousand years, at least for 800 to 900 years. Nalanda was subjected to depredation several times before being finally ruined by the marauding hordes of Bakhtiyar Khilji.

Nalanda, as built by Shakraditya, must have come into great prominence as an educational centre because his son Buddhagupta Raja, and his successor Tathagatagupta Raja, added more colleges to the existing ones, responding to the growing needs of the institution. Rulers of different dynasties—the Guptas, the Vardhamanas, the Maukharyas, the Palas and the Senas—played pivotal roles in the university's development, maintenance and preservation.

Xuanzang on Nalanda

Xuanzang gives a succinct account of Nalanda's growth and development. He mentions that Shakraditya, King Kumaragupta I, founded the sangharama at Nalanda. When he ascended the throne after him, Buddhagupta Raja continued to labour at the excellent undertaking of his father. To the south of the existing structure, he built another sangharama. Tathagatagupta Raja also vigorously adhered to the rules of his ancestors and built another sangharama to the east of the existing one. Baladitya ascended the throne next and built a sangharama on the northeast side. He also built a great vihara about 300 feet high. Due to its magnificence, dimensions and the statue placed within it—according to Xuanzang—it resembled the great vihara built under the bodhi tree.

Xuanzang further stated that King Baladitya's son Vajra, who inherited the throne, was 'possessed of a heart firm in faith.' The King Vajra that Xuanzang speaks of has been identified with King Vikramaditya II, the son and successor of Baladitya Raja, also known as Narasimhagupta. He built a sangharama to the west side of the convent. After this, 'king of Central India built to the north of this great *sanghârâma*... He built around these edifices

a high wall with one gate. A long succession of kings continued
the work of building, using all the skills of the sculptor, till the
whole was truly marvellous to behold.'[44] King Harshavardhana of
Kannauj appears to be the 'king of Central India'.

It is clear from Xuanzang's account that King Harshavardhana
openly favoured Buddhism. It is, therefore, not surprising that a
king like him would build a sangharama to propagate Buddhism.
Moreover, Harsha was the only king of Central India who, on
account of his supremacy, could stretch a hand of charity to a
place as distant as Nalanda. No other king would dare to do it.
Harsha must have built the sangharama after he had defeated King
Shashanka, who reigned in the seventh century and was the greatest
oppressor of Buddhism after Mihirakula.

Harsha not only built a great sangharama at Nalanda but also
constructed a vihara with brass plates and a high wall around all
the buildings. He helped and encouraged the university in several
other ways as well. Numerous students and professors had to be
maintained by the institution. In addition to the provision of food
and raiments for them, Harsha took upon himself the feeding of
some 40 priests daily as a special charge to show his gratitude to
the founder, as the Chinese visitor says.

There was still another way in which the university received
help from Harsha. Wherever he went and whatever his other
professions might have been, he championed and upheld Nalanda's
religious and philosophical doctrines. For instance, while touring
through Odisha, he came across some learned Hinayanists who
ridiculed him for having built a vihara at Nalanda which, they
said, believed in the 'sky flower' doctrine, representing the illusory
nature of existence. But Harsha asserted the superiority of this
doctrine over that of the Hinayanists, and to prove this, sent a
messenger to Nalanda with a note to Shilabhadra, asking him

---

[44]Xuanzang, *Si-yu-ki: Buddhist Records of the Western World Book IX*, Samuel
Beal (trans.), Routledge, California, 2008, p. 170.

to send four monk scholars for a debate he had organized for this purpose.

Although not as exhaustive as Xuanzang's, I-Ching's account of the place fully corroborates his predecessor's findings. About the first royal founder of the Nalanda buildings, I-Ching states that the Nalanda temple was built by Shakraditya (Kumaragupta I) for Raja Bhoja, the bhikku of North India. Apparently, after commencing construction, he was obstructed by other people, but his descendants completed it and made it the most magnificent establishment in Jambudvipa. The building comprises four squares, with four large gateways of three storeys each. Each storey is about 10 feet high. The entire temple is covered with tiles.

The Establishment and Growth of Nalanda

The question now arises: When was Nalanda built? The Sanskrit scholar and archaeologist Hasmukh Dhirajlal Sankalia, working through epigraphic material, has also said, as stated earlier by Xuanzang, that the earliest date assigned to Shakraditya is 415–416 CE.[45] It appears that the king was a Shaivite at the time he ascended the throne. Another inscription, however, states that he was a Buddhist, and the date recorded there is 448–449 CE. Therefore, we can safely assume that the king's religious views underwent a change between these years. He must have built the sangharama at Nalanda to propagate Buddhist learning and to prove that he was a devout Buddhist. However, he would not have taken this step at the end of his reign in 450 CE. It must have been earlier. If his conversion came around 420 CE, then such a gesture can be expected from the king within five or ten years of his conversion, that is to say, in or around 425 CE. That is how 425 CE was assigned as the approximate date for the royal establishment of the university.

---

[45]Sankaliya, H.D., *The University of Nalanda*, Oriental Publishers, Delhi, 1972.

Apart from the royal Gupta patrons, excavations have also yielded seals of King Manasimha, seals of the high officials Pashupatisimha and Devasimha, seals of various offices such as head of a *vishaya* or *adhikaran*, or of officers in charge of various departments of administration, and *kumaramatya* or officials who aided in ruling the different provinces of the empire. Not all of them were Buddhists. Most were non-Buddhists, as the emblems of the public seals and those of the officials clearly show. Therefore, it can be said that the contribution of non-Buddhists to the continued maintenance of Nalanda and its large student population was important.

The Destructive Fire

Nalanda seems to have gone through a tragedy at the end of the fifth century CE, as certain areas of the premises were destroyed by fire. Although there is no written evidence in the form of inscriptions or archaeological evidence, burnt debris in the deeper layers of Monastery Number One suggests these buildings were destroyed by fire at the end of the fifth or beginning of the sixth century CE. Two independent accounts corroborate this: one Indian, almost contemporary, and the other Tibetan.

A Sanskrit Buddhist work, *Manjushrimulakalpa*, talks of a foreigner named Gomi who entered India through Kashmir, destroyed many monasteries and killed several monks. However, Gomi's identity is in doubt. According to Taranath, a Persian king, Ban-de-ro alias Khun-ma-ripta, ruled in Multan and Lahore. Several wars and treaties were recorded between him and King Dharmachandra. During peace, this Persian king destroyed Magadha due to a misunderstanding caused by monks and Brahmins, 'ruined many temples, and heavily damaged Shri Nalendra. Even the ordained monks fled away.' Then King Buddhapaksha, son of Dharmachandra's maternal uncle, an ardent Buddhist, 'reconstructed all the damaged temples' and invited the monks back. 'In Sri Nalendra, eighty-four centres of the Doctrine were established. Of these, seventy-one were established by the king and the remaining by the queen and the ministers.' His son Gumbhirapaksha followed suit and dug several tanks and wells.

Xuanzang, in his account of the construction of the university, does not stop with Harsha, for he says, 'A long succession of Kings continued the work of building.' Harshavardhana died in 647 CE without leaving an heir. Chaos ensued as different dynasties fought with each other to gain control over Magadha. So, it is believed that the University received no royal patronage until the advent of the Palas around the year 750 CE. However, the Yashovarmanadeva inscription belonging to the king of the same name was found in Nalanda. He probably ruled Kannauj from 725–757 CE or 728–745 CE, though the dates vary in different sources. He supported the Mahavihara, as did the Maukharis.[46] Xuanzang speaks of one Purnavarma, who presented to Nalanda a 'figure of the Buddha standing upright and made of copper, 80 feet in height,' and to cover which he constructed a six-tiered pavilion. Some scholars have surmised this Purnavarma to be the last of the Maukharis.

In the middle of the eighth century, the Palas emerged from the political chaos in Bengal as elected rulers. Gopala was the first elected emperor of the Pala Dynasty in 750 CE. Because of the turbulent times in which he came to acquire the Pala throne, he could not do much for Nalanda, although, according to Tibetan tradition, he founded a monastery. The Empire peaked during the reign of Gopala's son, Dharmapaladeva, a disciple of Jnanapada. Dharmapala was a great patron of Buddhism. He studied the *Prajnaparamita* (The Perfection of Wisdom) and some sections of

---

[46]Pandey, Naina, 'The Nalanda Stone Inscription of Yashovermadeva', *The Heritage of Nalanda*, in C. Mani (ed.), Aryan Books International, New Delhi, 2008, pp. 68–69.

the *Kriya* and *Yoga tantras*; he built a monastery called Amritkar to the south of Nalanda.

Dharmapaladeva, too, must have patronized the university in one way or another, as a copper plate discovered at Nalanda indicates. However, it is so hopelessly defaced that nothing can be made out beyond 'Dharmapaladeva' inscribed on a seal soldered at the top and engraved in one line below the Dharma Chakra (symbol of the wheel of law), and the fact that it was issued from the royal camp. He donated 200 villages to Nalanda to revive it after the political upheaval, during which it received no grants for several years. He is also credited with founding the University of Vikramshila, probably on Patharghat Hill, near Bhagalpur, a city on the banks of the Ganga, because he felt that Nalanda had passed its prime. Vikramshila later evolved into a great learning centre of Buddhism. Emperor Dharmapala established another university at Sompura (also known as Paharpura or Varendra), now in Bangladesh. Tibetan tradition also attributes the foundation of the monastery at Odantapuri to him, but this claim has been challenged.

Emperor Ramapala, the fifth in the line of Pala kings, was the last strong Pala ruler. He is said to have gained control over Kamarupa and Kalinga and founded the Jagaddala University.

The university is situated in the village of Jagdal in Dhamoirhat Upazila, northwest of present-day Bangladesh, on its border with India. These five universities—Nalanda, Vikramshila, Odantapuri, Sompura and Jagaddala—formed the network of the five great Buddhist universities.

The Testimonies of Inscriptions

Dharmapaladeva was succeeded by his son Devapala, who was also a staunch supporter of Buddhism and seems to have entirely identified with the cause of Nalanda. Two inscriptions from his time bear testimony to how famous the university had become.

The first is the Nalanda copperplate of Devapaladeva, and the second is the Ghoshrava inscription. According to the first, King Balaputradeva of Suvarnadvipa, 'attracted by the manifold virtues of Nalanda and through devotion towards Buddha, he erected there a vihara, and having received the aforementioned five villages as a result of entreaties through his ambassadors, from king Devapala, made a gift of them...'[47] Balaputradeva had requested King Devapaladeva, through one of his ambassadors, to grant five villages—Nandivanaka, Manivataka, Natika, Hasti and Palamaka—towards the income of the blessed Lord Buddha, the abode of all virtues, like tagging a perimeter for offerings, oblations, shelter, garments, and so on of the assembly of the venerable for the upkeep and repair of the monastery when damaged. It is remarkable that King Balaputradeva of the far-off Suvarnadvipa and Yavadvipa, the modern islands of Sumatra and Java, should have decided to patronize Nalanda. The plate further states, 'This Balaputradeva is now known to be one of the rulers of the Shailendra dynasties,' who had built up an empire in Southeast Asia in the eighth century. This patronage was of no mean degree, consisting of a monastery and the grant of five villages for its maintenance and preservation. Therefore, King Balaputradeva can be counted in the same distinguished category of kings as Kumaragupta I, Narasimhagupta and Harshavardhana, who contributed to the rise of Nalanda and gave it a unique position among the centres of learning.[48]

The Ghoshrava inscription bears evidence of another kind. According to it, Devapaladeva received the very learned Brahmin, Viradeva, who had come to Nalanda after visiting many learning

---

[47]Majumdar, N.G., Monograph of the Varendra Research Society, Rajshahi Nalanda Copperplate of Devapaladeva, *Inscriptions of Bengal Volume III*, April 1926, p. 6.

[48]Sahai, Bhagwant (Dr), *The Inscriptions of Bihar (From earliest times to middle of 13th century A.D.)*, Archaelogical Survey of India, Patna, 1983.

centres such as Kanishka Vihara and Yashovarmmapura. Viradeva was elected head of Nalanda afterward at the assembly of monks. This indicates that King Devapaladeva was probably connected with the administration of the university, and this, in addition to the profound learning of Viradeva, was perhaps the reason why the learned Brahmin was elected head of the sangha.

After Devapala, the next king to patronize Nalanda was Gopala II. However, his rule over Magadha was very short, so he probably could not do much for Nalanda except give it some donations. The resurgence of the Pala Dynasty came after Mahipala I ascended the throne (988 CE) and with his reconquest of Magadha. And Nalanda once again found a royal patron who could substantially contribute to it. He is said to have constructed two temples and repaired several monuments at Nalanda after a fire damaged or destroyed them. In the eighth or ninth year of Mahipala's reign, a great temple, perhaps the Temple of Baladitya, was burnt down. Although Mahipala did not repair and restore it himself, the temple was rebuilt in the eleventh year of his reign by a person named Baladitya from Tilodaka, or modern Telhara, who had migrated from Kaushambi.

The next reference to a Pala king and Nalanda comes from the time of Rampala (1082–1124 CE), the fifteenth ruler of the Pala Dynasty, who had to face periods of alternate success and defeat. Govindapaladeva was perhaps the last Pala king to patronize Nalanda because after he died in or around 1197 CE, the various dynasties—Chahamanas, Gahadavalas, Palas and Senas—that had long been contending over the spoils of Magadha were exterminated by the violent storm of the invasion of Bakhtiyar Khilji; Nalanda too met a similar fate.

However, even after Bakhtiyar Khilji conquered Bihar, some local Hindu or Buddhist rulers continued to govern small tracts of the country under the Khiljis. Mention has been found of King Budhadena, who according to Dharmasvamin, the Tibetan monk who travelled to India between 1234 CE and 1236 CE, belonged to the family of the maternal uncles of the Buddha. He ruled in southern Magadha, where Gridhrakuta, Rajagriha, Veluvana, Vajrasana or Bodhgaya, and Nalanda were situated. But the effects of Bakhtiyar Khilji's raids were evident everywhere. Bodhgaya was deserted and only four monks were found staying there. Even they fled when rumour spread that the Turushka (Turkic) soldiers were about to attack. The conditions at Nalanda were no different. About two days' journey southeast of Vajrasana, the Turkish soldiers damaged the buildings, and there was absolutely no one to look after them or make offerings. However, the indomitable spirit of Nalanda still prevailed in a venerable 90-year-old learned monk, the Mahapandit Rahulshribhadra, who continued to live there together with four other pandits and students.

The Glory of Nalanda Mahavihara

Nalanda was the university of universities. It was a place to which all aspired to come for instruction. What made it so sought after? It was located in a place with a long religious and educational tradition. It was the *karmabhumi* of both the Buddha and Mahavira. Great scholars such as Nagarjuna and Aryadeva were associated with it before it was established as a true mahavihara. It had a grand infrastructure built by successive kings and enjoyed continued royal patronage for almost 800 years of existence— including from foreign kings—except for about 100 years. As Xuanzang points out, while there are myriad sangharamas in India, Nalanda is the 'most remarkable for grandeur and height.'[49]

While all monasteries followed the rules of conduct and discipline given by the Buddha and were enshrined in the *Vinaya Pitaka*, according to I-Ching, these were followed with greater severity at Nalanda than elsewhere. The rules of the *Vinaya* are

---

[49]Li, Hwui, *The Life of Hiuen-tsiang*, Samuel Beal (trans.), Kegan Paul Trench Trubner and Company Limited, London, 1914, p. 112.

stipulations and advice that guide the sangha of monks and nuns. They are generally regarded as the basis of monastic life. Only because these were followed meticulously that life was regulated, serene and harmonious. Most importantly, the teachers of Nalanda were of excellent calibre and their fame as scholars was widespread within and outside India. I-Ching emphatically states that the uninterrupted prosperity of the monastery was entirely due to the monks strictly observing the rules of the *Vinaya*. I-Ching, who spent ten years here, gave a detailed insight into life at Nalanda.

Infrastructure

Xuanzang gives a glowing description of the monastery. Its beauty must have stunned anyone who saw it for the first time.

> [...] (T)he whole establishment is surrounded by a brick wall, which encloses the entire convent from without. One gate opens into the great college, from which are separated eight other halls, standing in the middle (*of the Sanghârâma*). The richly adorned towers and the fairy-like turrets, like pointed hilltops, are congregated together. The observatory is seen to be lost in the vapours (*of the morning*), and the upper rooms tower above the clouds.
>
> From the windows, one may see how the winds and the clouds (*produce new forms*), and above the soaring eaves, the conjunctions of the sun and moon (*may be observed*).
>
> And then we may add how the deep, translucent ponds bear on their surface the blue lotus, intermingled with the Kie-ni (*Kanaka*) flower, of deep red colour, and at intervals, the Âmra groves, spread overall their shade.
>
> All the outside courts, in which are the priests' chambers, are of four stages. The stages have dragon-projections and coloured eaves, the pearl red pillars, carved and ornamented, the richly adorned balustrades, and the roofs covered with

tiles that reflect the light in a thousand shades these things add to the beauty of this scene.[50]

It is no wonder that Nalanda was so beautiful, as a long succession of kings had built colleges and viharas for the monks. But more relevant is the fact that the physical and architectural grandeur of Nalanda was well-matched with the quality of learning imparted within.

As Xuanzang further says, 'The priests dwelling here are as a body, naturally (or, *spontaneously*) dignified and grave, so that during the 700 years since the foundation of the establishment, there has been no single case of guilty rebellion against the rules.'[51]

Sustenance in Abundance

When Xuanzang reached Nalanda, he was given all the essentials he might need. He received 120 *jambiras* or lemons daily, 20 areca nuts, 20 nutmegs, an ounce of camphor and Mahashali rice. This special rice—each grain as large as a black bean—grew only in Magadha. When cooked, it was extraordinarily aromatic and shining. It was only offered to the king or religious persons of great distinction. Xuanzang seems to imply, however, that all visiting priests were treated very well, as he goes on to explain that in the Nalanda convent, the abbot entertained a myriad of priests in this fashion. Besides the Master of the Law, there were men from every quarter; in all their wanderings, these men did not receive such courteous treatment anywhere else.

According to Xuanzang, 10,000 priests and lay people lived and studied in Nalanda. They not only studied Mahayana Buddhism but also the works of all 18 schools of Buddhism, the Vedas and other books, the *Hetuvidya, Shabdavidya, Chikitsavidya,*

---

[50]Ibid., 111–112.
[51]Ibid., 112.

the works on magic, the *Atharvaveda*, and the philosophy of *Sankhya*. Besides these, they also thoroughly investigated other miscellaneous works. About a hundred pulpits were arranged every day for preaching, and the students attended these discourses punctually without fail. I-Ching talks of over 3,000 monks who lived in Nalanda, as opposed to Xuanzang's figure of 10,000, and the former is generally accepted as a more realistic figure.

Organization and Administration

Considering the large number of monks living at Nalanda and the intense study and religious practices that they were engaged in, the university had to be meticulously organized and administered. Arpita Chatterjee gives details of the management of the Nalanda Mahavihara through epigraphic material.[52] Travel accounts of Xuanzang and I-Ching also show that several rulers gave Nalanda Mahavihara many land grants for maintenance. According to Xuanzang, Nalanda Mahavihara owned a hundred villages. By the time I-Ching came to Nalanda, some 30 years after the return of Xuanzang in 645 CE, the number of villages granted to the institution had increased to no less than 200. All these villages must have been in the neighbourhood of the mahavihara.

The administration of the granted villages was usually the responsibility of the grantees, so Nalanda Mahavihara must also have been responsible for administering the villages given to it. How did the mahavihara manage these villages? Chatterjee points out that some neighbouring villages remained connected with the main administrative units, and the revenues were transferred to the mahavihara. She points to 13 seals discovered at Nalanda belonging to different village assemblies or grama sabhas, among

---

[52]Chatterjee, Arpita, 'Management of Nalanda Mahavihara from Epigraphic Material', *The Heritage of Nalanda*, in C. Mani (ed.), Aryan Books International, New Delhi, 2008, pp. 74–76.

which are villages connected to Nalanda. The seals show that the villages were ruled by their village assemblies and were a source of income for the mahavihara. This also means that Nalanda Mahavihara was not concerned with the villages' day-to-day administration. This arrangement must have suited the monks as they could reap the benefits of the land grants without having to shoulder the administrative responsibilities.

However, there remained the problem of revenue collection. Xuanzang talks of 200 householders from a hundred villages who contributed several hundred piculs (a unit of weight equalling the amount a man can carry on a shoulder pole—about 60 kilograms) of ordinary rice and several hundred catties (two catties are about one kilogram) of butter and milk every day, indicating that these 200 householders were responsible for collecting the revenue from the villages. They could be either members of gram janapadas or middlemen securing Nalanda Mahavihara's interest in lieu of some payment. They were entirely responsible for the timely collection of revenues. This arrangement was also beneficial for both parties as the mahavihara regularly received articles of daily need, and the middlemen earned a profit through the collection process.

However, this could not have been true of all the villages, as many of them were donated to the monastery with full administrative powers. There are indications that the mahavihara looked after at least some villages in the neighbourhood. The Nalanda copperplate of Devapaladeva shows the grant of complete ownership of five villages to Nalanda Mahavihara, with their pasture lands, grounds, spaces, mango and mahua trees, waters and dry lands, and all taxes due to the king.[53] According to I-Ching, there were many monasteries in India where the monks themselves supervised the cultivation, and this may have been the case with the Nalanda Mahavihara.

---

[53]Sharma, Archana, 'The Nalanda Copper-Plate of Devapaladeva', in C. Mani (ed.), *The Heritage of Nalanda*, Aryan Books International, New Delhi, 2008, pp. 71-72.

This raises the question of whether monks were allowed to engage in agriculture, trade and commerce according to the rules of the *Vinaya*. I-Ching explains that the *Vinaya* accepts procurement of subsistence as a right to livelihood, that the ploughing and weeding of fields had to be done appropriately, and that sowing and planting had to be done without violating the guiding principles of the religion. If food was taken according to the regulations, there was no blame, and one could honestly say that one was increasing one's happiness by building up the body.

According to the *Vinaya*, when the sangha of monks cultivate the paddy fields, they must share the crops with the monastic servants. It may also share them with other families responsibile for cultivating the fields. They were entitled to one-sixth of the produce. The sangha only provided farm cattle and land and was not responsible for anything else. Hence, it could also adjust the division of the crops appropriately according to the circumstances.

Despite the *Vinaya* regulations, some monks transgressed. They were greedy and did not share the produce with others in the required proportion. They employed male and female slaves and managed the farming business personally. The monks who abided by the disciplinary rules refused to eat the food produced by such monks because they considered the personal running of a farm by a monk to be an improper livelihood. By ordering about the hired men working in the fields, they inevitably aroused their resentment, and digging up the earth to plant seeds as well as ploughing land was liable to injure ants and other insects. They questioned why such an evil deed should be done for food. Hence, an honest and upright monk would be disgusted by the cumbersome task of farming. He would rather go far away with his pot and bowl to sit quietly alone in a forest, in the lap of nature. Being away from the hubbub of pursuing fame and gain, he would cultivate the calm of nirvana. However, it was permitted in the *Vinaya* for a monk to manage a business to gain profit for the sangha as long as he did not cultivate land or injure living things. When I-Ching arrived at Tamralipta for the first time, he saw a square field outside the monastery. Some laypeople suddenly came there to fetch vegetables, which they divided into three portions, giving one portion to the sangha and taking two portions away for themselves. He did not understand what was happening and asked the venerable Mahanadip about it. Mahanadip replied that the monks of the monastery observed disciplinary rules by which they were not allowed to cultivate the land themselves. They could lease the land to others and take a share of the crops for food. They could thus sustain their lives and, at the same time, free themselves from the guilt of destroying living things by ploughing and irrigating the fields.

Internal Management of the Mahavihara

The mahavihara required an organizational and administrative structure for its internal management. The Nalanda Mahavihara was a conglomeration of many monasteries. According to Xuanzang, six monasteries were built by six kings, and a brick wall surrounded all the buildings. Ruins of 11 monasteries have been found at the excavated site. Each of these monasteries had management that dealt with all its internal matters.

Available records show that an apex committee was tasked with looking after the entire campus and the bhikku sanghas of different monasteries served under its supervision. Many seals, apparently of the apex committee, have been discovered here. Seals from other monasteries have also been found. The Nalanda stone inscription of Yashomarmadeva tells of Malada, the son of a minister, who gifted food along with clarified butter, curds and other such goods, as well as a lamp, to the bhikkus of all quarters. What is interesting is his gift of an *akshay nivika* to facilitate regular worship at the monastery. Akshay nivika is like what we know today as a fixed deposit. The interest accrued on it was used to meet the approved expenditure. The bhikku sangha was expected to manage the akshay nivika itself. Therefore, the bhikkus engaged in some financial activities with this amount, mainly to increase the interest earned from it to benefit the sangha. The seals discovered also reveal the existence of several departments for the management of affairs. For example, *nava karmika* bhikkus oversaw the construction and repair of buildings on campus. Another set of bhikkus oversaw provisions such as clothes and grains, and many maids and servants serviced the viharas. Therefore, apart from religious and educational activities, there were departments of banking, stores and kitchens in each monastery of Nalanda, all coordinated by the apex committee. This committee also looked after the welfare and necessities of the pilgrims, who could purchase various items of worship from the stalls run by the bhikku sangha. The Nalanda stone inscription of Yashomarmadeva shows that the donors purchased various items from such stalls or *sanghattikas* to give gifts to the bhikkus.

At the head of the whole organization was the chairman, whose decision was the ultimate decision on each matter. Since he was the supreme authority of the institution, special, qualified persons were needed to fill this post, as can be seen from the appointment of outstanding scholars such as Shilabhadra and Viradeva. The Ghoshrava inscription (a stone inscription from the Buddhist ruins in this village near Nalanda) also posits that this person had to be selected as per the collective decision of all the members of the sangha. This was possibly to ensure that all members acquiesced to the chairman's authority and leave little room for discontent and dissension.

Admission and Curriculum

Since I-Ching came primarily to study the *Vinaya* rules and stayed in Nalanda for ten years, he gave a more meticulous account of life at Nalanda than Xuanzang.[54] According to him, two kinds of students were admitted to the university—those who had completed their basic education from Nalanda and those who had studied elsewhere and sought admission to Nalanda for further education. The mahavihara admitted both those who wanted to pursue a secular career and those who wanted to be ordained as monks. Once they became students at Nalanda, both had to follow the same rules. For those already studying at Nalanda, admission was a natural progression after their basic education had been completed. Others were examined by an eminent scholar who guarded the portals of the university and questioned the aspiring student to test his knowledge. They ensured that only the most deserving entered Nalanda. According to I-Ching, out of every ten examined, only a couple succeeded, and seven or eight were rejected. All accounts suggest that the examination must have been rigorous. Students of moderate talent were not only bound to fail to get admission, but their exclusion even forfeited their fame as eminent debaters. However, for the students who received their primary and secondary education at Nalanda and often embraced Buddhism, no such examination was necessary. They first had to study the works of their faith and system. Then, over time, when they had finished certain works, they were placed in charge of various departments of the university.

The Primary Curriculum

What was Nalanda's primary and secondary education like? This is important because at least this much knowledge was expected of aspirants who came from outside and sought admission to Nalanda. I-Ching gives an elaborate account of the curriculum and teaching methodology.

---

[54]I-Tsing, *A Record of Buddhist Religion as Practised in India and the Malay Archipelago, AD 671–695,* J. Takakusu (trans.), Delhi, Munshiram Manoharlal, 1998.

Great emphasis was laid on *shabdavidya*, or the knowledge of words, and according to I-Ching, all over India, secular books in general were known as *vyakarana* or grammar, of which there were five principal works to be studied:

1. *Siddhavastu* **or spelling book:** Also known as *Siddhirastu*, this was an initiatory book for beginners in primary school, dealing with the 49 letters of the alphabet, multiplied and arranged in 18 sections totalling over 10,000 syllables, comprising over 300 stanzas. There were four lines in each stanza, and each consisted of eight syllables, making 32 syllables in a stanza. The stanzas could be short or long. Children began learning this book at the age of six and completed it in six months. The book was said to be composed by Maheshvara (a name for Lord Shiva), which means the book was composed so far back in time that the author was unknown.

2. *Sutra:* These explained the rules of grammar. The groundwork of all grammatical writings, the *Sutra* consisted of 1,000 stanzas composed by the great scholar Panini. He is said to have been inspired and aided by Maheshvara in writing this work, and when the latter opened his third eye, the people of his time believed that this was really the case. Eight-year-old children could complete its study in eight months.

3. *Dhatu* **or verbal roots:** This book also had 1,000 stanzas to explain grammatical roots.

4. *Khila,* **the book of** *khilas* **or supplementary works:** Khila means wasteland; the metaphor refers to the wasteland reclaimed by a farmer. The three khilas were the *Ashtadhatu,* the *Munda* and the *Unadi.* I-Ching gives an exhaustive description of these texts; however, in brief, they can be described as follows:

   a. *Ashtadhatu:* This deals with the seven cases and the ten tenses and moods of a finite verb and explains the 18 personal terminations of verbs and nouns. All nouns possess seven cases, each with three numbers—singular, dual and plural. Thus, there are 21 forms for each noun altogether. Besides the seven cases, there is the evocative case, which is the eighth one. Just like the first case, the other cases also have three numbers. This means that each noun has 24 inflections. The technical term for the inflected noun endings, according to the case, was *subanta*. The ten tenses denote the ten grammatical terms used to express the three different tenses of a verb. The 18 terminations indicate the first, second and third person in the three numbers of a verb. These 18 terminations are collectively called *tinanta*.

b. *Munda*: This talks about the formation of compound words. For instance, the Sanskrit word for tree is *vriksha*, which can be used to form more than 20 compounds by combining it with other words to create the names of other objects related to trees.

c. *Unadi*: This is roughly the same as the *munda*, except that what is fully explained in the one is only briefly mentioned in the other. A ten-year-old child needed to study hard for three years to grasp the meanings of the three khilas.

5. *Vritti Sutra*: This is a commentary on Panini's *Sutra*, on which quite a few commentaries have been written. It consists of 18,000 stanzas elucidating the text, with a detailed explanation of the manifold meanings and normative values of the universe that govern both gods and humans. The *Vritti Sutra* was composed by the scholar Jayaditya, a man of great ability and literary talent. It is said that he could understand everything he heard once without having to learn it again.

A 15-year-old child could understand the book after studying it for five years. Having mastered this commentary, the student could proceed to learn the composition of letters and memorials submitted to emperors, write poems, devote his mind to the study of *hetuvidya* or logic, and pay attention to the *Abhidharma-Kosha-Shastra* (an encyclopaedic compendium of *Abhidharma*, scholasticism). By poring over the *Nyaya-Dvara-Tarka-Shastra* (the science of dialectics, logic, and reasoning), he learnt to draw inferences in the right way, and by reading the *Jataka Mala*, his fine talent was developed.[55]

This takes the basic education to the age of 20. The emphasis on the study of Sanskrit and its grammar is ironic, as the Buddha seems to have been emphatic that his teachings should be made available to the people in their language. A story is recounted in the fifth section of the *Cullavagga* (selected texts elaborating on the etiquette and duties of the bhikkus, as well as the rules and procedures for addressing offences that may be committed within the sangha). Once, two Brahmins, Yemulu and Tekula, came to the Buddha and, sitting at a respectful distance, told him that the monks corrupted his speech by using their dialects. They wanted to offer his teachings to the people in the metrical form of the Vedas (by which they probably also meant that the teaching would be in Sanskrit). The Buddha rebuked them by saying, 'Foolish men, how can you suggest such a thing? This will affect people's confidence...' After rebuking them, Buddha said, 'You shouldn't give metrical form to the word of Buddha. If you do, you commit an offence of wrong conduct. You should learn the words of the Buddha using its expressions.'[56] There has

---

[55]Ibid., 169–175.
[56]Brahmali, Bhikku, 'Theravada Collection on Monastic Law: The Small Division: The Chapter on Minor Topics', *SuttaCentral*, https://tinyurl.com/monastic-law. Accessed on 29 October 2024. *The Book of Discipline, Vol. V, (Cullavagga),*

been controversy over such extensive use of Sanskrit in Buddhist texts. One reason put forward is that without the knowledge of Sanskrit, the Brahmin pandits of Vedic learning could not be defeated. The second is that the people, who were used to learned men using Sanskrit, could not be persuaded to accept the teachings of the monks in their language. Whatever the reason, a thorough knowledge of Sanskrit—its grammar and usage—was an essential prerequisite for education at Nalanda and other reputed monasteries.

Higher Education: The Study of Sanskrit Grammar

After this basic education, a student could enter the realms of higher learning at a university like Nalanda or Vallabhi, where he would receive instruction from a tutor for two or three years. This initial grounding was necessary to proceed to other texts, some described below.

Apart from the *Vritti Sutra*, Patanjali, the renowned ancient scholar, composed another commentary on Panini's *Sutra* titled *Churni*. This commentary consisted of 24,000 stanzas. In this work, Patanjali analyses the frame and structure of Panini's *Sutra* and fully elucidates the *Vritti Sutra*. It takes at least three years to study and understand Panini's *Sutra*.

Then there is the *Bhartrihari Shastra*, a commentary on *Churni*, composed by the great scholar Bhartrihari in 25,000 stanzas. It deals extensively with the essentials of human affairs and grammatical knowledge, and relates the causes of the rise and fall of various families in great detail. Bhartrihari, according to I-Ching, was profoundly learned in the theories of *Vijnapti Matra*, or consciousness, and was well-versed in syllogisms. His reputation resounded all over India. According to I-Ching, Bhartrihari was a Buddhist, a fact many scholars have refuted.

I.B. Horner (trans.), The Pali Text Society Oxford, 2011, pp. 193–194.

I-Ching also talks of him as a contemporary of the great Buddhist scholar Dharmapala but then contradicts himself when he says that Bhartrihari died 40 years earlier.

There is also the *Vakyashastra*, or *Vakyapadiya*, composed by Bhartrihari, in 700 stanzas—with a commentary of 7,000 stanzas—giving a description of argumentation based on the authority of the sacred teachings and of inference by comparison, as in syllogisms. The next work ascribed to Bhartrihari by I-Ching is the *Vital* (*Vritta*) in 3,000 stanzas, with a commentary of 14,000 stanzas. According to him, the main body of the work was composed by Bhartrihari and the commentary was by the renowned Buddhist scholar Dharmapala. According to I-Ching, only a man whose learning had reached the stage of studying this book could be said to have mastered the science of grammar. All these books had to be studied by both monks and laymen for them to be considered well-informed scholars.

The importance of studying grammar is illustrated by the experience of Dharmasvamin, a Tibetan monk of the thirteenth century, who thought he knew grammar better than many people in Magadha. But when he came to Nalanda, he found many young disciples studying grammar with Guru Rahulabhadra. The guru advised him to study the Sanskrit commentary and master it. Dharmasvamin had the humility to acknowledge that he benefited from this, which helped him understand the whole meaning of the texts.

Those praised as excellent scholars at the university became famous far and near for their abilities. They could aspire to serve at the king's court after proving their knowledge through suggestions and debating prowess. They acquired such expertise that they could ultimately defeat their opponents in debates, another Buddhist school or Brahmin. Their fame resounded throughout the entire realm and beyond. They received feudal estates, were promoted to high ranks, and were entitled to write their names in white, high on the gates of their houses.

Xuanzang gives a detailed account of his study of Sanskrit grammar at Nalanda. He heard the explanation of the *Yoga Shastra* thrice, the *Nyayanusara Shastra* and the *Hin-hiang-tui-fa-ming* once, the *Hetuvidya Shastra*, the *Shabdavidya Shastra* and the *Tsah-liang Shastra* twice, and the *Pragyamula Shastra-Tika* and the *Shat Shastra* thrice. The *Kosha, Vibhasha*, and *Shatpadabhidharma Shastras* he had already heard explained in different parts of Kashmir. Still, when he came to this university, he wished to study them again to clear his doubts. Once this was done, he also devoted himself to studying Brahminical books and the work called *Vyakarana* on Indian letters, an ancient text whose authors were unknown. In his description of the text, Xuanzang traces it back to its hoary past and divine authorship:

At the beginning of each Kalpa, Brahma-râja first declares it and then transmits it for Devas and men to use. Being thus declared by Brahma-râja, therefore, men call it *Fan*, or Brahmâ, writing. The words of this book are very extensive, comprising hundred myriad ślôkas. It is the same as the old commentary called the Vyâkara(*na*)-śâstra. But this pronunciation is not complete. If correct, it would be, which is "another name for a treatise relating to the record of the science of sounds." It treats at large, in a mnemonic way, on all the laws of language and illustrates them, hence the name.

At the beginning of the Kalpa of perfection (*vaivarta kalpa*), Brahma-râja first declared this book; it then comprised 100 myriad ślokas; afterwards, at the beginning of the *Vaivarta-siddha-Kalpa*, that is, the kalpa, or period of establishment, Ti-shi (*Śakra-raja*) reduced them to ten myriad ślôkas. After this, a Brahmin of the town Śâlâtura in Gandhâra of North India, whose name was Pânini Rishi, reduced them to 8000 ślôkas. This is the work at present used in India.

Lately, a Brahmin of South India, at the request of a king of South India, reduced them further to 2500 ślôkas.

This work is widely spread, and is used throughout all the frontier provinces, but the well-read scholars of India do not follow it as their guide in practice. This then is the fundamental treatise relating to sounds and letters of the Western world, their branch-divisions, distinctions and mutual connections. Again, there is a Vyâkaraṇam work (*mnemonic treatise*) of a short kind having 1000 ślôkas; again, there is one of 300 ślôkas on the roots (*bases*) of letters (*i.e. letter roots or bases*); again, there are (*treatises on the*) two separate kinds of letter-groupings, one named Maṇḍaka, in 3000 ślôkas, the other called Uṇâdi in 2500 ślôkas. These distinguish letter-groupings from letter-roots. Again, there is the treatise called Ashta-dhâtu (*Dhâtu vṛitti?*) in 800 ślôkas; in this work, there is a brief conjunction of letter-bases and letter-groupings. These are all Vyâkaraṇa treatises.[57]

After this, Xuanzang goes on to give a more detailed explanation of the grammar contained in these books, which he studied thoroughly.

From the accounts of Xuanzang and I-Ching, it is emphatically understood that knowledge of Sanskrit was essential for all bhikkus—whether Buddhists or Hindus—who wanted to pursue their studies in universities. Not only the grammar but also the use of the language was essential and had to be understood. Students had to realize that words both conceal and reveal. For this, they had to learn to combine their knowledge of language with the concepts of Dharma. According to I-Ching, the supreme truth is far beyond the reach of words or speech, but the worldly principles of concealment are not apart from wording. He explains that the term 'worldly principles' was formerly known as 'worldly truth',

---

[57]Li, Hwui, *The Life of Hiuen-tsiang*, Samuel Beal (trans.), Kegan Paul Trench Trubner and Company Limited, London, 1914, pp. 121–122.

but this did not fully express its meaning. The correct meaning is that ordinary matters conceal essential truths. The material clay, for instance, is not originally a pitcher. Still, people erroneously think of it as a pitcher. And the sound of a human voice does not contain any song, yet people mistake it for the essence of a song. Perception, at the time of its formation, is non-distinctive, and it is due to the covering of ignorance that various forms illusorily take shape. However, since people do not understand the nature of their minds, they think that the perceived object exists outside the mind. Both the snake and the rope that causes the illusion of a snake are false conceptions. When the right knowledge is hidden away, the truth is concealed, which is why it is known as the worldly principle of concealment. The word 'concealment' implies worldly, hence the term 'worldly concealment'. Or one can say veritable truth and concealed truth.

Based on his experiences at Nalanda, I-Ching advised that the people of China coming to India should acquire knowledge by studying the works he described. Otherwise, their labours would be fruitless. He said that all these books should be memorized, but only men of higher talent could do this. Others might only understand the meaning. Of the students at Nalanda, those who wished to become monks were called 'children of men'. Those who sought only secular learning were merely called students. According to I-Ching, both classes of pupils had to provide food for themselves. This, however, is disputed by most scholars. Xuanzang says, 'Students here, being so abundantly supplied, do not require to ask for the four requisites. This is the source of the perfection of their studies, to which they have arrived.'

Those who wished to be ordained could do so immediately upon entering Nalanda. According to I-Ching, after being ordained, the disciple did not have to make offerings to others. But if his teacher had the means, he could prepare some gifts on behalf of his disciple—such as a girdle or a strainer—for the monks who had to be present at the altar during the ceremony.

Then the *upadhyaya*, or spiritual teacher, gave the disciple the text of the disciplinary rules and taught him the character of the offences and how to recite the rules. When the disciple had learnt them well, he would read the full text of the *Vinaya Pitaka*, or the collection of books on monastic discipline. He had to recite them every day and try to always conduct himself accordingly or risk losing his determination. While studying the *Vinaya Pitaka*, he began to learn the sutras and shastras.

The Status of Monks

After receiving full ordination, the monk was called a *dahara* monk or junior monk. When he had passed ten full summer retreats, he was known as *sthavira* or elder. As a monk with ten years of standing, he could leave his teacher and abide by himself. He might also act as an upadhyaya. When a monk wrote letters or communicated with others, he had to clarify whether he was a dahara, a sthavira, or a *shramanera*. If he was well-learned in Buddhist and secular literature, he could call himself a *bahushruta* (one who has heard a lot). This indicates that the teaching methodology was essentially oral. A bhikku, however, could never call himself a sangha because it referred to a group of at least four monks. Hence, an individual couldn't use this term for himself. To be an upadhyaya, one must be a sthavira, having passed ten full summer retreats. There was, however, no seniority requirement for the *karmacharya* who acted as a private tutor, and for monks who served as witnesses; only that they must be well-learned in the *Vinaya* and faithfully observe its disciplinary rules. If one had to take the name of his teacher, he had to respectfully say that he was only saying it out loud because circumstances required him to do so before mentioning his name.

Teaching Methods

From the records of Xuanzang, it seems that the same teaching method was adopted in most cases. The teacher helped the student in his studies by explaining the various difficult passages of the book. The leader of Nalanda, Shilabhadra, taught the *Yogacharabhumi Shastra* to Xuanzang and other audiences three times in nine or 15 months.

Xuanzang also learnt from Jayasena, a householder and lay Buddhist scholar who lived on the mountain called Yashtivana. As a youth, Jayasena first studied the *Hetuvidya Shastra* under Bhadraruchi, a master of shastras, and then the *Shabdavidya Shastra* and other texts of both Mahayana and Hinayana under Stithmati Bodhisattva. He also studied the works of secular writers: the four Vedas, works on astronomy and geography, medicinal art, magic and arithmetic. He mastered these from beginning to end, and there was no field of knowledge in which he did not have expertise. He was known far and wide for his accomplishments. Once, Purnavarma, the king of Magadha, invited Jayasena to his court and nominated him Master of the Kingdom, assigning him the revenue of 20 large towns for his support. But Jayasena respectfully declined both the honour and the revenue. After Purnavarma's death, when Shiladitya became king, he again invited Jayasena to honour him as the Master of the Country and assigned to him the revenue of 80 large towns of Odisha. However, once again, Jayasena declined the offer, saying:

> Jayasêna has heard that he who receives the emoluments of the world (*men*) also is troubled with the concerns of life, but now my object is to teach the urgent character of the fetters of birth and death; how is it possible then to find leisure to acquaint myself with the concerns of the king?[58]

---

[58]Ibid., 154.

With these words, he bowed respectfully and departed; the king could not detain him. From then on, he lived constantly in Yashtivana, where he took charge of disciples, teaching and leading them to persevere and expound the books of the Buddha. Several hundred laymen and priests honoured him as their master. Xuanzang stayed with Jayasena for two years and studied the treatises on the difficulties of the *Vidyamatra-siddhi Shastra* and several others. He also asked him for explanations of passages in the *Yoga Shastra* and the *Hetuvidya Shastra,* about which he still had doubts.

Apart from the tutorial method, discussions were held in which students acquired knowledge by listening and participating. These discussions were held from morning till night. Xuanzang and I-Ching seemed to have been very impressed by this part of the activities at Nalanda. Although there were some subjects, mainly about the religious side of Buddhism rather than the philosophical, on which lectures were delivered, even these lectures often took the shape of personal discussions between the teachers and the students who could not follow the lecture or had doubts about some topics.

It is not known whether the students had to do written assignments. But they certainly had to copy the manuscripts, of which the *Prajnaparamita* was the most important. Epigraphic evidence shows that copying manuscripts was one of the students' most important activities. Xuanzang and I-Ching took hundreds of manuscripts from India and copied many of them, perhaps at Nalanda.

The prime method of sharpening the student's cognition and memory was to insist on repeated and careful reading; this helped the student understand and memorize the words. By doing this diligently for ten days or a month, thoughts became clear, leading to clear articulation of concepts and arguments. As I-Ching states, 'After a long practice of ten days or a month, a student feels his thoughts rise like a fountain and can commit to memory whatever he has heard once (not required to be told twice).'[59] Therefore, teaching at Nalanda was primarily done through tutorials, the effort being to sharpen the intellect and bring out the best in the student. For this, emphasis was placed on individual attention according to the needs of each student.

Teacher–Student Relationship

I-Ching is emphatic that the instruction of pupils was the most important factor in the prosperity of Nalanda. If due attention was not paid to the teaching-learning processes, it would lead to the extinction of the university. Hence, all precautionary measures had to be continually taken to maintain the excellence of teaching and learning 'so that it doesn't slip off as a fish from the net'. This led to great emphasis being placed on the teacher-student relationship and interaction. I-Ching details how the two were expected to behave towards each other. The Buddha had prescribed the regimen in the *Mahavagga*.

I-Ching says that the manner of conduct had been handed down in India since antiquity. According to the rules, the pupil should go to his teacher for the first and last watch of the night. The teacher first invited him to sit comfortably and then taught him a suitable passage from the *Tripitaka*, leaving no fact or theory unexplained. He examined the moral conduct of his pupil to prevent him from committing mistakes and violating the disciplinary rules. Whenever he realized his pupil had committed a mistake, he advised him to repent and confess. Then, the pupil massaged his teacher's body, folded his robes tidily, sometimes swept the room and the courtyard, and inspected the water to see that no insect had fallen in before sending it to the teacher.

---

[59]I-Tsing, *A Record of Buddhist Religion as Practised in India and the Malay Archipelago, AD 671–695*, J. Takakusu (trans.), Delhi, Munshiram Manoharlal, 1998, p. 183.

He did whatever had to be done in order to show his respect for the teacher.

Great emphasis was placed on personal health and hygiene. The *Vinaya* instructed every pupil to chew toothwood early every morning and then come to his teacher to offer him toothwood, *gleditsia* (used as soap), water and the towel, which had to be kept at the sitting place. Once these things were properly arranged, he had to worship the holy image of the Buddha, walk around the shrine hall and then return to his teacher's seat, where, after tidying up his robe, he had to say a salutation without standing up. Putting his palms together, he had to touch the ground with his head three times, and—while kneeling on the ground, with his head bowed and hands joined—say, 'May my upadhyaya be attentive!' He could use the word acharya instead of upadhyaya. He then goes on: 'Now I beg to enquire whether the upadhyaya slept well last night, whether his four elements of the physical body are in peace and harmony, whether he is ready to take his morning meal.' These enquiries could be lengthy or brief, according to circumstances.

The teacher answered the queries according to convenience. Then, the pupil went to the adjoining rooms to salute his seniors. Just as the etiquette between teachers and students was carefully regulated, so was that between junior and senior students, probably to avoid personal clashes. I-Ching writes that the rites of salutation were also practised according to the Buddha's teachings. The seniority of a monk was determined by the time he received full ordination, which further determined whether he was entitled to be saluted by his juniors. The Buddha said that there are two kinds of men worthy of being saluted—the Tathagata (the one who has attained Buddhahood) and the senior bhikkus. When a junior monk saw a senior one, he would politely express respect, uttering the word *vande* (in praise) while prostrating before him. The senior monk might remain standing at this time. If he was already seated, he could sit up straight with his hands in front and say *arogya,* or 'may you be healthy'. If this exchange didn't happen, they would both be at fault.

The student sat with his teacher, read a short section of scripture, and memorized what he had learnt before. He had to study new lessons daily and review what he had learnt earlier without wasting a moment. He was also required to wait until after daybreak before seeking permission from his teacher to have the morning meal. I-Ching explains that a student could not eat porridge before dawn without asking his teacher's permission, without chewing wood, without ascertaining that the water for his daily use was free of insects, and without washing and cleaning himself. There were protocols for all these activities. An elaborate description is given of the way the teeth and tongue were to be cleaned, and the mouth rinsed. Water had to then be passed through the nostrils in the prescribed way, and those who couldn't do this could drink water before eating anything.

The cleanliness of water was also a matter of great importance. A whole process was given and the water had to be examined carefully to ensure that there were no insects in it, even the tiniest ones. If required, it could be strained using a thin cloth or a strainer. It was an essential part of a bhikku's equipment. If the water had been kept overnight for use, it had to be examined and strained again in the morning.

For bathing, I-Ching says, 'There are more than ten great pools near the Nalanda monastery, and there every morning, a *ghanti* is sounded to remind the priests of the bathing-hour. Every one brings a bathing sheet with him. Sometimes a hundred, sometimes a thousand (priests) leave the monastery together and proceed in all directions towards these pools where all of them take a bath.'[60] He further describes the proper way to take off clothes and wear the bathing skirt to ensure that no monk is totally exposed at any point of time.

---

[60]Ibid., 108–109.

When receiving full ordination, the pupil, after shaving his head and putting on the plain robe of a homeless monk, needed to ask his teacher for permission to do anything. For instance, before taking a meal, the pupil had to go to the teacher to seek permission. After saluting him according to the rules, he asked the teacher, 'May my upadhyaya be attentive! Now I ask your permission to wash my hands and alms bowl to take a meal.' The teacher was wont to respond with, 'Be careful about it!' Permission for other such tasks was sought in the same way. After considering the matter and the time required, the teacher might give or withhold permission. If the pupil had many things to do, he could ask permission to do them all at once. However, this was not strictly in accordance with the *Vinaya* rules. Further, permission had to be sought clearly, and the request worded lucidly. As a student was generally required to seek his teacher's permission, he would not normally question the student. Hence, it was up to the student to be true to his dharma.

The student was exempt from seeking permission for the most personal things, like performing ablutions and going for *chaitya vandana*. I-Ching explains chaitya vandana thus:

It is said that when the Buddha entered nirvana, men and gods assembled to cremate his remains. They collected fragrant firewood and built a funeral pyre. This place was known as *chiti*, meaning pile, which gave rise to the name *chaitya*. It was built by piling up bricks and earth. As it was assumed that all of Buddha's virtues were accumulated here, it was an object that inspired meditation. It was also called a stupa. *Vandana* means salutation—a way of paying respect to one's superiors with a sense of humility. The mode of salutation is detailed in the *Vinaya*. Briefly, when one went to pay homage or ask permission from their teacher, he had to drape his religious robe properly. The robe and skirt had to be held in such a way that they did not touch the ground when kneeling, with the two heels pointing upwards and the back and neck forming a straight line. The ten fingers were spread on the ground before bowing the head, and no part of the robe or anything else was to be used as padding under the knees. This prostration had to be repeated with one's hands joined palm to palm. In this manner, one piously made salutation three times. However, ordinarily one salutation was sufficient and no rule required it to be repeated.

If there was dust on one's forehead, he could rub it off with his hand and then wipe it clean. Next, he had to wipe off the dust on his knees, and after adjusting his robe, he had to sit to one side or stand for a while. The senior monk usually asked the pupil to take a seat, but if the pupil was reprimanded, he had to remain standing. If several senior monks were to be present, several seats were prepared for them. All this was done according to the *Vinaya*.

No large couches were provided in the lecture halls and dining rooms of the monasteries. Still, many blocks of wood and small chairs were prepared for the monks to sit on while listening to a lecture or having a meal. In China, I-Ching points out, monks were accustomed to sitting cross-legged on big couches.

If the pupil fell ill, the teacher personally attended to him and gave him medicine, feeling the same anxiety that he would feel if the pupil were his child. But according to the guiding principles of the Buddha's teachings, instruction and edification were foremost, and love and anxiety should not blind the teacher to them. Just as a monarch attended to fostering and educating his eldest son, so too the teacher had to prepare his student for life.

All activities in the monastery were regulated by time, for which water clocks or clepsydras were kept in all large monasteries. They were accurate devices for measuring time and were donated by successive generations of kings and watchers so that the monks always knew the hour. The lower part of the device was a copper vessel filled with water, on which a copper bowl floated. The bowl was thin and delicate, capable of holding two *sheng*s (litres) of water. At its bottom was a tiny pinhole through which water flowed. When the bowl was full of water, it sank, and a drum was sounded. Commencing at dawn, one stroke of the drum was sounded at the first sinking of the bowl, two strokes at the second sinking, and three strokes at the third sinking. After four strokes of the drum at the fourth sinking, a conch shell was blown twice, ending with another drumbeat, indicating the first hour, when the sun rose in the east. After the second round of the bowl-sinking, the drum was sounded twice to indicate the second hour; this marked the exact moment of high noon. When the drum was struck twice, the monks had to stop eating. If anyone was found still eating, he was expelled from the community, according to monastic regulations. In the afternoon too, there were two hours announced in the same way as in the forenoon. The four hours of the night were like those of the day. A day and a night consisted of eight *pahar*s (each three hours long in the present sense of the term).

At the end of the first watch, the director of duties struck the drum in the monastery's loft to announce the time for the monks. Both at dusk and dawn, the drum was beaten at the gate for a stretch. Servants or porters performed these miscellaneous affairs. From sunset to dawn, neither the ordinary monks nor the servants were allowed to sound the drum or a bell. The director of duties had to do this himself. This was the routine at Nalanda. However, different monasteries had different ways of keeping time. In Kushinagara, for example, the bowl sank sixteen times between dawn and midday. It was due to the use of clepsydras that no one was ever perplexed about noon, even on a dark, cloudy day. To enable the director of duties to perform his duties efficiently, he was allowed to keep a small clepsydra in his chamber. And even when it rained, he was allowed to leave the clock on during the night to sound it effectively, and the hour was always known. A skilful mechanic was required to regulate the device correctly by adding or removing water from the bowl as the length of days and nights varied according to the seasons.

The End of Study

It took a pupil five summers to master the *Vinaya*, after which he could leave his teacher to travel the world to pursue other subjects of study. However, wherever he went, he needed to depend on a teacher for learning. It was only after the completion of ten summer retreats that he could be independent. However, if a monk did not become conversant with the *Vinaya*, he would need a teacher for the rest of his life. If no senior teacher was available, he had to stay with a junior one and behave towards him in the same way as towards a senior teacher, except for offering a salutation to him. He also did not need to enquire about his teacher's health every morning and evening or ask whether he had lived up to the rules of the *Vinaya*.

Therefore, the monks were supposed to learn all the *Vinaya* texts and research the scriptures and commentaries to enable them to defeat heretics in debates and solve queries as easily and as naturally as ice melts in boiling water. In this way, they became famous throughout the country and were more respected than ordinary men. It was as if they were helped by heavenly beings to spread their knowledge and guide all living beings to emancipation. I-Ching, however, concedes that there could only be one or two such outstanding persons in each generation who could be compared to the sun and moon and regarded as 'Naga elephants', considered the best elephants. There were such people as Nagarjuna, Aryadeva, and Ashvaghosha in the remote past. In the Middle Ages, there were Vasubandhu, Asanga, Sanghabhadra, Bhavaviveka and others. In more recent times, there were Dinnaga, Dharmapala, Dharmakirti, Shilabhadra, as well as Simhachandra, Sthirmati, Gunamati, Pragyagupta, Gunaprabha, Jinaprabha, and so on. These great teachers embodied various religious and secular virtues, being self-contained men of little desire.

Dharmakirti was a great teacher of *Hetuvidya*, while Gunaprabha brought glory to the study of the *Vinaya* texts.

Gunamati engaged in the practice of meditation, according to the school of Dhyana, and Pragyagupta laid down the distinctions between truth and heresy. These teachers could write a composition as swiftly as the echo of a sound. They did not need to take the trouble to study the 10 classics in full, nor did they need to repeat the book 100 times in two volumes, being able to understand what they had heard once.

5

The Decline of Nalanda

The growth and glory of Nalanda were spectacular. The university was an unparalleled landmark on the map of Asia. But as mercurial and dramatic as its growth was, so was its decline. It was not due to a single event or cause but a process that lasted centuries. While Nalanda was finally destroyed in 1193 by the marauding forces of the Turkish leader Bakhtiyar Khilji, its decline began much earlier, sometime after the rise of the Pala Dynasty in Bengal, which also ruled over Magadha.[61] The journey of the university can be divided into two phases—one from the sixth to the ninth centuries, when it grew and developed along the liberal cultural traditions inherited from the Gupta Age, and the second in the Pala period from the ninth to the thirteenth centuries.

Internal Factors for the Decline

Among the key factors that played a role in the progressive change and decline were Tantrism and ritualism entering the university curriculum in a big way, thus killing its austere discipline and subsequent intellectual growth. The Pala kings were Buddhists, but as votaries of Tantrism, they encouraged Tantric learning in the university. Apart from the development of Tantric thought, there

---

[61]Dutt, Sukumar, *Buddhist Monks and Monasteries of India: Their History and Their Contribution to Indian Culture*, Motilal Banarsidass, Delhi, 2015, pp. 344–348.

was competition between Brahminism and Buddhism which had always existed, but gradually Brahminism became more powerful and dominant. The Palas tried to counter the Brahmanical challenge by establishing other centres of Buddhist learning, such as Odantapuri, Vikramshila, Sompura and Jagaddala. This took away much of Nalanda's sheen. It also resulted in diminishing the exclusive royal patronage of Nalanda as resources had to be distributed among all institutions.

The backbone of the Buddha's teaching was service to the people and the propagation of his thoughts among them in a language and manner they could comprehend. Once the university received land grants from the kings and became affluent, the monks no longer needed to go out for alms. This caused a disconnect between the people and the monks. Since the university mainly received land grants for its maintenance, it effectively became a landlord, and a feudal structure developed to manage the land revenue. This must have further distanced the monks from the laypeople, which was the strength of Buddhism.

It has also been said that as the monasteries grew, Buddhism withdrew into them and abstruse doctrines were developed and written in the elite Sanskrit language. As Taranath points out, the monks themselves were corrupted as the mahavihara fell on troubled times.

Tantric Influences

By the time the Palas came to the throne, Mahayana itself had become heavily embedded with the Tantric cult, and Vajrayana Buddhism had become widespread. Odantapuri became far more popular than Nalanda, being the seat of Tantric learning. Vikramshila also became a great centre of Buddhist learning and culture, but the emphasis on Tantra was evident. There were 53 cells suitable for Tantric esoteric practices and 54 rooms for the general use of monks, totalling 108 chambers around the

Central Monastery. Nalanda followed suit, as can be seen in the images of many Tantric deities recovered from the site. During this period of Tantric predominance at Nalanda under the Palas, this centre of liberal learning fell from its standards of liberal scholarship. It became more and more a centre of studies in Tantric doctrines and magic rites. Its strength as a centre of intellectual learning, leading to its fame in the east and Tibet, was lost and limited to its area.

The Pala Dynasty and the Tibetan Perception

The history of Nalanda during the Pala period was primarily written by Tibetans who came to India at the time of Xuanxang. The Indo-Tibetan exchange replaced the Sino-Indian interaction around the eighth century, when the number of Chinese monks coming to India petered out after a steady flow. Liang Chi Chao mentioned 180 monk pilgrims from China in his essay, 'Chinese Students Going Abroad 1500 Years Ago and Afterwards.'[62] I-Ching wrote about the lives of fifty-one monks. Most of them belonged to impoverished families, except four or five, whose fathers and grandfathers held imperial posts.[63] Buddhism was the religion of the elite, developed by a group of cultured and intellectual monks who excelled in both Buddhist and secular learning. But by the sixth and seventh centuries, Buddhism had spread to the masses and was firmly established by this time in the society of the Tang Dynasty. This must have led to Chinese monks trying to reach India to study Buddhism at its origin. I-Ching writes of the travails of the journey and the challenging conditions even after reaching India:

---

[62]Ibid., 297.

[63]I-Ching, *Chinese Monks in India: Biography of Eminent Monks who went to the Western World in search of the Law during the Great Tang Dynasty*, Latika Lahiri (trans.), Delhi, Motilal Banarsidass, 2015.

When I left China, I had fifty companions, but when I reached the Western Country, only two or three were left. There was not a single Chinese Monastery there. Because there was no fixed place (for us), we had to move from place to place like grass swept by the wind. Under such difficult circumstances, to study Buddhism and the Law is really a very great effort.[64]

It is no wonder that after over three centuries of Chinese monks coming to India, the exuberance and enthusiasm was over. However, Indian monastic scholars, who must have faced similar difficulties, continued to travel to China, braving the harshness of the journey until much later. They introduced the prevailing Tantric Buddhism of India to China, but even with them, the excitement was finally over.

The interaction with Tibet began with the Tibetan King Sron btsan-sgam-po or Songstsen Gampo, who, under the influence of his Chinese Buddhist wife, sent his minister Thonmi Sambhota to Nalanda in the early seventh century. Sambhota, who returned to Tibet after a course of study, must have given a glowing report of what he had seen and learnt at Nalanda, for the king converted to Buddhism and declared Buddhism the state religion for the first time in Tibet. Sambhota is also credited with remodelling the Tibetan language on the principles of Sanskrit grammar. It is not known who the others who followed him were. Still, Nalanda became a symbol of excellence for the monastic establishments in Tibet engaged in studying and learning philosophy. In 1359 CE, a monastery named Nalanda was founded in Tibet, which also housed a school of philosophy filled with monks of different sects. They could safely stay, study and preach there without interruption, instead of wandering around the country.

---

[64]Dutt, Sukumar, *Buddhist Monks and Monasteries of India: Their History and Their Contribution to Indian Culture*, Motilal Banarsidass, Delhi, 2015, p. 312.

The Tibetan monastery seems to be modelled on Nalanda's liberal cultural traditions.

The Tibetan accounts supplement those of the Chinese. For example, information about the three grand libraries of Nalanda—Ratnadodhi, Ratnasagar and Ratnaranjita—in Dharmaganj on the Nalanda campus comes from the Tibetan records. Since Nalanda was the long-established surviving mahavihara, it must have had a wealth of manuscripts, both original works and copies of sutras and shastras. The king of Sumatra, who built a monastery in Nalanda, gave the revenue of five villages to be used not only for the maintenance of the monks but also for copying the manuscripts. There must have been numerous manuscripts in Nalanda Monastery, but few have survived.

Tibetan legends say that the founder of the Pala Dynasty, Gopala, founded a mahavihara of grand proportions in the newly built city of Odantapura (Odantapuri), only about six kilometres from Nalanda. It was known to the Arabs as Adwand Bihar and is today's Bihar Sharif. At the time of the foundation of the Odantapuri Vihara, Nalanda still enjoyed its fame and prestige. Still the development of other centres of learning must have drawn many learned monks away from Nalanda. Tibetan writings speak of the migration of scholars from one mahavihara to another. Thus, Nalanda became one of many rather than the only one. Atisha, the great Buddhist master, is said to have been ordained at Nalanda but went to Odantapuri for further studies. This sounds strange, considering the premier position that Nalanda held. He eventually became the abbot of Vikramshila Monastery before being escorted to Tibet. By this time, Nalanda was way past its glory.

During the earlier Gupta period, the leadership of Nalanda was reserved for eminent scholars of liberal learning and of broad philosophical outlooks, like Dharmapala and Shilabhadra. But later, the Palas looked for another kind of learning and exercised a much greater say in the appointment of the head.

This explains why King Devapala commissioned the learned Brahmin Viradeva to look after Nalanda. Taranath said that the head of Vikramshila also controlled Nalanda. In the narratives about the lives of eminent Buddhist saints and scholars that Taranath intersperses in Tibetan history, he refers to Vajrasena as head of the different centres of learning at Gaya, Nalanda, Odantapura and Vikramshila. Taranath writes about the eminent *siddhas* and Tantra gurus who taught the Tantric cult. This work contains the life story of the famous Pandit Abhayakaragupta, who rose in the reign of King Mahipal of the Pala Dynasty (reigned 988 to 1038 CE). He became the abbot of all three premier monasteries—Mahabodhi, Nalanda and Vikramshila.[65]

Buddhism Challenged by Brahminism

Societally, the time had come for the decline of a centre of Buddhist learning as Buddhism in North India dwindled. It retained its strength in eastern India but in northern India, it was challenged by Brahminism. The tension had always been there, and it has been well-documented. Abhishek Kumar, bringing together different points of view, articulated the strategies adopted by both the Buddhists and the Brahmins to establish the predominance of their traditions in the regions of Gaya and Bodhgaya. The contest was between Vaishnavism, Shaivism and Buddhism. The worship of Surya was incorporated into Vaishnavism, as Surya was seen as a form of Vishnu. Vaishnavism and Shaivism, too, found it easy to come together to contest Buddhism. The sangha tried to build a significant grassroots following by dotting the landscape with Buddhist shrines and narratives of their sanctity, linking them to different phases of the Buddha's life. This was a way of bringing Buddhism to the people without necessarily having to

---

[65]Taranatha, *History of Buddhism in India*, Lama Champa and Alaka Chattopadhyaya (trans.), Motilal Banarsidass Publishers, Delhi, 2018, pp. 289–293.

travel to the major places of worship. As these shrines had to be maintained and resources were required for them, however small, this was also a way of securing donations for the sangha. This served to maintain the sangha even when the large centres withered away due to a lack of funds.

The Vaishnavas declared Gaya a place of sacred funerary rites as early as the first century CE but it had become well-established by the fifth and sixth centuries. They also appropriated the Buddhist shrines and described them as Vaishnava shrines, including those considered the holiest of the holy by the Buddhists. For example, the Brahmins claimed the Bodhi tree under which Buddha is said to have obtained enlightenment. Xuanzang encapsulates the Buddhist perception of the shrine:

> In the centre of the enclosure is the Diamond Throne, which was perfected at the beginning of the Bhadra Kalpa and rose up the ground when the world was formed. It is the very central point of the universe and goes down to the Golden Wheel, from whence it rises upwards to the earth's surface. It is perfected of diamond and is almost 100 paces round...1000 Buddhas of the Bhadra Kalpa have all attained their emancipation here....(T)he place of complete wisdom is also called the arena of wisdom (*Bôdhimanda*).[66]

The Gaya Mahatmya in *Vayu Purana* presents an entirely different account of the same place because it describes it as sacred to the Hindus. According to mythology, Vishnu took the form of a child during the cosmic flood and slept soundly on a branch or leaf of the imperishable banyan tree. The present banyan tree is believed to be a mythic tree.[67]

---

[66]Li, Hwui, *The Life of Hiuen-tsiang*, Samuel Beal (trans.), Kegan Paul Trench Trubner and Company Limited, London, 1914, pp. 103–104.

[67]Singh, Rana B., 'Sacredness and Manescape: The Sacred Geography of Gaya, India', Ashok K. Dutt, Vandana Wadhwa, Baleshwar Thakur and Frank J.

Thus, since pre-Buddhist times, the Bodhi tree has been identified as a Vaishnava place, which has also been done in Puranic literature. The cult of the Vaishnava order, established in the wider Bodhgaya region in the fourth and fifth centuries, enjoyed significant importance in the post-Gupta period. In the eighth century, Vaishnavism burgeoned in Gaya. Shiva was the other god prominently present in the region. Numerous sculptures of Uma-Maheshvara were found here. From the sixth century onwards, Pashupata Shaivism seems to have spread through Pashupata ascetics, who established Shaiva monasteries and shrines and received the royal patronage of the Vardhanas, Maukharis, and other rulers.

Counteracting Strategies

The Buddhists adopted two strategies to counter Vaishnavism and Shaivism—contesting through debate and hierarchical appropriation of Brahminical religion, including Buddhist temples. Xuanzang cites two instances of debates between the Brahminical orders and the Buddhist monks, which form the background for constructing the Gunamati Vihara and Shilabhadra. In both stories, the heretics, probably the Shaivas, were defeated in debate by the Buddhist monks. These victories made the local kings appreciate the wisdom and intellect of the Buddhist monks, who then requested that each of the two monks involved establish a monastery. The kings also donated villages to support the new monasteries. These stories not only indicate the fierce competition between Hindu ascetics and Buddhist monks but also show the significant stakes involved. Victory in the debate ensured the establishment of new monasteries and

Costa (eds.), *Facets of Social Geography: International and Indian Perspectives*, Foundation Books published for Cambridge University Press, India, Delhi, pp. 502–525.

land grants for sustenance, whereas defeat brought ignominy and the withdrawal of royal support.

The second strategy of hierarchical appropriation of Vaishnavism and Shaivism by the Buddhists is found in the narratives of Xuanzang and Dharmasvamin, the last Tibetan monk to come to Nalanda. The Buddhists said that a follower of Maheshvara built the Mahabodhi Mahavihara. According to their accounts, the small Ashokan shrine at Bodhgaya was reconstructed in the Mahabodhi Mahavihara by two Shaiva Brahmin brothers who were instructed by none other than Maheshvara himself to construct the mahavihara to acquire copious merit in a superior religious field. By saying that Maheshvara or Shiva instructed the Shaiva Brahmins to construct a Buddhist mahavihara, it implies that Buddhism was superior to Shaivism as a religion. This was an attempt to create a hierarchy. The importance of the Bodhi tree in generating merit and being more beneficial to the pilgrim than even Mount Kailash was also a way of garnering donations.

Another instance of the Buddhist attempt to establish hierarchical superiority over Brahminical religions is found in the concept of Trailokyavajra, both in the sculptural and textual traditions. The story of Trailokyavajra is about the subjugation of Rudra Shiva by Heruka. In brief, the story narrates the emanation of one of the bodhisattvas, Vajrapain, as Heruka (wrathful deity), who becomes angry with Maheshvara and vanquishes him. Maheshvara accepts his defeat and submits to Heruka. After this submission, Heruka resurrects Shiva and his consort as Uma. Maheshvara gives them a new name, Bhairava-Bhairavi, and admits them into the Buddhist fold as powerful lay followers.

Once the Hindu deities were incorporated into Buddhism as subordinate deities, they were installed in the Buddhist monastic complexes and village shrines. This must also have been a way of attracting the Maheshvaras, or the ordinary Shiva devotees, who were then encouraged to make donations to these Buddhist establishments. Therefore, the Buddhist response to Vaishnavism and Shaivism was lengthy and complex. The process also had to be justified and explained in accordance with Buddhist doctrine and theological positions. In effect, it required a re-articulation of Buddhist doctrines and led to the development of a redefined Buddhist order.

Even when royal patronage to Nalanda was at its peak, the Gupta kings were mostly Vaishnavites and not Buddhists, although they allowed both Jainism and Buddhism to flourish freely. Even the greatest king of the Vardhana dynasty, Harshavardhana, an ardent supporter of Nalanda and its Mahayana doctrine, was not a Buddhist. If Xuanzang's account of his charity in Prayag is weighed carefully, it shows that he gives far more to the Brahmins than the Buddhists. Xuanzang, who was present at the time, writes:

On the first day of this period, they installed the image of the Buddha within one of the thatched buildings on the field of charity. They then distributed precious articles of the first quality and clothing of the same character and offered exquisite meats whilst they scattered flowers to the sound of music. At the close of the day, they retired to their tents.

On the second day, they installed the image of Âditya-deva and distributed precious things and clothing in charity to half the amount of the previous day.

On the third day, they installed the image of Iśvara-deva and distributed gifts as on the day before.

On the fourth day, they gave gifts to 10,000 of the religious community, arranged in a hundred ranks. Each received 100 pieces of gold, one pearl, one cotton garment, various drinks, and meats, flowers and perfumes. After the distribution, they retired.

The fifth arrangement was the bestowal of gifts to the Brahmans, which lasted for 20 days.

The sixth turn related to the heretics, which lasted 10 days.

The next occasion was the bestowal of alms on those who came from distant spots to ask for charity: this lasted for 10 days. The eighth distribution was to the poor and the orphans and destitute, which occupied a month. By this time the accumulation of five years was exhausted. Except the horses, elephants, and military accoutrements which were necessary for maintaining order and protecting the royal estate, nothing remained.[68]

The Decline of Patronage

With the rise of the Rajputs from the tenth to the twelfth centuries, donations to the mahaviharas were diverted towards Brahminical establishments more so than before. However, there are scattered references to grants to Buddhist monasteries. Since earlier grants were supposed to be in perpetuity, these monasteries did not face immediate financial crises. The Gahadavalas, who ruled in the eleventh and twelfth centuries, were supposed to be the last patrons of Nalanda and other Buddhist establishments. The attempts of King Govindachandra and his queen, Kumaridevi, to revive the glory of Nalanda are significant. King Jaichandra, who ruled from 1170 to 1192 CE, was a disciple of a Buddhist monk, but he was known as a worshipper of Lord Krishna. Most of the Gahadavala kings adopted the title of Parameswaran. An examination of the Gahadavala grants shows that most of these grants, including those from villages, went to Brahmins, marking a clear shift in the nature of donations. Thus, grants that Buddhist institutions had earlier received were now given to the Brahminical sects and their institutions. These general trends in the shift of patronage must have also impacted a large establishment like Nalanda.

---

[68]Li, Hwui, *The Life of Hiuen-tsiang*, Samuel Beal (trans.), Kegan Paul Trench Trubner and Company Limited, London, 1914, p. 186.

Monarchs, republics, nobles and wealthy businesspeople had always patronized Buddhism. When this patronage waned, the institutional decay of the Buddhist monastic system began, and Nalanda was no exception. Villages donated to Nalanda may have led to the feudalization of Nalanda's management. The majority view is that the proper establishment of the university began to take shape in the age of Shakraditya (Kumaragupta I). I-Ching says that the Indian monasteries possessed special allotment of land, from the produce of which the monks' clothing was to be supplied, and that the priests or laymen in the monastery could obtain goods from the same source by virtue of the donor's original intention. Although some monasteries had great wealth, granaries full of corn, and many male and female servants, money and treasures hoarded in the treasury were not used. Therefore, the monks had to live in poverty. There were some monasteries which, according to I-Ching, did not provide food for the residents but divided the produce amongst the senior monks and made the other monks arrange for their food; such monasteries also did not allow strangers to reside there. Some viharas possessed so much property and were so powerful that they began to not only issue their seals and coins but also wield considerable power and influence in their respective localities.

Some monks may even have been involved in revenue disputes, cases and petitions, which distanced the monks from the laity and prompted the Turks to invade these monasteries for their wealth. By now, therefore, the upkeep of large monastic establishments was no longer in consonance with the thought process of the people, both the rulers and the ruled. Large-scale 'monkship' was no longer tenable, and the students coming out of the mahavihara did not know what to do with themselves in society. They could neither stay in the monastery nor find gainful employment at court. Therefore, when the final blow came, the only reason why Nalanda could not be resurrected was that, by then, times had changed.

Invasion and Destruction

The attacks on Nalanda were not new. It had been subjected to depredation several times before, but after each one, it had always regained its original position. The final blow came with Bakhtiyar Khilji, from which the university would never recover, although its flame of survival gasped for a while before being completely extinguished.

Before the marauding hordes of Bakhtiyar Khilji, there had been others. No sooner had Nalanda been founded by Shakraditya and expanded by his son Buddhagupta and his successor Tathagatagupta than it was destroyed by Mihirakula, the ruler of the Alchon Huns of Central Asia who invaded Central India in the early sixth century. Then came the fire that destroyed sections of the university complex at the end of the fifth century or the beginning of the sixth century.

Manjushrimulakalpa, a Buddhist work in Sanskrit, tells of a foreigner named Gomi who entered India through Kashmir, destroyed many monasteries and killed several monks. However, Gomi's identity is disputed. According to Taranath, a Persian king, Ban-de-ro alias Khun-ma-ripta, ruled Multan and Lahore. Several wars and treaties were recorded between him and King Dharmachandra. During a period of peace, this Persian king destroyed Magadha due to a misunderstanding caused by monks and Brahmins. He 'ruined many temples and heavily damaged Shri Nalendra. Even the ordained monks fled away.' Then King Buddhapaksha, the son of Dharmachandra's maternal uncle, an ardent Buddhist, 'reconstructed all the damaged temples' and invited the monks back. 'In Sri Nalendra, eighty-four centres of the doctrine were established. Of these, seventy-one were established by the king himself and the remaining ones by the queen and the ministers.' His son, Gumbhirapaksha, followed suit and dug several tanks and wells.

It has been argued that despite the sizeable Buddhist population in the northwestern part of the Indian subcontinent,

Bengal and Magadha were the first to take the heat of the Turushka atrocities. Afghanistan and Kashmir had a sizeable number of Buddhist monasteries in the early medieval age. Bakhtiyar Khilji, a native of Afghanistan, was well aware of such matters. Further, his assignments in Bihar gave him ample opportunity to exploit the resources of the Buddhist establishments. The political void in Magadha and the famed opulence of the monasteries may have been the reason for this. All such early invaders believed that the Buddhist monasteries possessed huge amounts of wealth, and hence, it was not that they mistook the monasteries as military strongholds, as some scholars claim. Still the opulence of the monasteries caused enormous damage to them.

The policy of dividing the spoils of war between the king and the soldiers, which the early Sultanate rulers had followed in the Indian subcontinent, must have been responsible for the plundering and destroying of the viharas. Not only Bakhtiyar Khilji himself but also the Turushka soldiers were engaged in the looting. Dharmasvamin, who was in India from 1234 to 1236 CE, has given a short but very valuable account of the state of Magadha and of Nalanda, where he spent about six months. He was a very learned man who had acted as an interpreter for the monks Shakyashri, Buddhashri and Ratnashri. In his introduction to Dharmasvamin's biography, Roerich explains that the Turushkas had not established any stable administrative machinery except at Bihar Sharif, where they had military headquarters. Hence, the soldiers roamed around Magadha, causing consternation among the people with threats and exactions. Taranath says:

> The Persians at last built a fort on the ruins of Odantavihara. Dharmasvamin himself got a taste of it. When he was returning to Tirhut, he met two such soldiers in the ferryboat across the Ganga, who demanded gold from him, and when he threatened to complain to the king, they became wild and snatched away his begging bowl. Fellow travellers of

Dharmasvamin tried to settle the matter by offering some ornaments, but they only relented when Dharmasvamin himself gave some money to them.

The political void in Magadha must have emboldened Khilji to plunder the monastic universities of Odantapuri, Nalanda and Vikramshila to augment his resources. His advance, however, was not unobstructed. According to Taranath, 'To protect Odantapurí and Vikramśíla, the king even converted these partially into fortresses and stationed some soldiers there.' He goes on to say, 'Then came the Turuṣka king called Moon to the region of Antaravedi in between the Ganʾgā and the Yamunā. Some of the monks acted as messengers for this king. As a result the petty Turuṣka rulers of Bhamʾgala and other places united, ran over the whole of Magadha, and massacred many ordained monks in Odantapurí. They destroyed this and also Vikramaśíla.' This shows that the Turushka sovereignty was already recognized and accepted. It is not clear who the king called Moon is. Harbans Mukhiya thinks it might refer to Shihab-ud-din Muhammad Ghori or Qutub-ud-din Aibak, but this is perplexing as Bakhtiyar Khilji's role in the destruction of Nalanda and the other viharas is well-known.[69]

As Taranath points out, Khilji's task must have become easier as the monks themselves had been corrupted, and many had become collaborators, acting as messengers for this king at the cost of their community. Taranath says, 'There is no doubt that many *siddhas* and *sādhaka*-s lived during this period. But since the *karma* of people in general was unalterable, all these could not be prevented. At that time, most of the *yogí* followers of Gaurakṣa (Gorakṣa) were fools and, driven by the greed for money and honour offered by the *tírthika* kings, became the followers of Íśvara. They used to say, "We are not opposed even to the Turuṣkas."'

---

[69]Taranatha, *History of Buddhism in India*, Lama Champa and Alaka Chattopadhyaya (trans.), Motilal Banarsidass Publishers, Delhi, 2018, pp. 318–319.

Premonitions and Prophecies of Destruction

Xuanzang had an eerie premonition about the destruction of Nalanda five centuries earlier when he was studying with Jayasena. Hwui Li's biography of Xuanzang says:

When this was done he unexpectedly dreamt in the night and saw all the chambers and courts of the Nâlanda monastery deserted and foul; moreover, there were nought but water buffaloes fastened in them, with no priests or followers. The Master of the Law entering through the Western gate of the hall of Bâlâditya râja, beheld on the top of the four-storeyed pavilion a golden coloured man, of a grave and imposing countenance, whilst a glorious light shone within the entire abode. His mind was overjoyed, and he wished to ascend to the top, but he found no way to do so; he then besought him to reach down and lift him up—but he replied; "I am Manjuśri Bôdhisattva; your karma does not yet admit of (*such a privilege*)"—and then pointing to the outside of the convent, he said: "Do you see that?" The Master of the Law looking in the direction indicated by his finger, saw a fierce fire burning without the convent, and consuming to ashes villages and towns. Then the golden figure said: "You should return soon, for after ten years Śilâditya râja will be dead, and India be laid waste and in rebellion, wicked men will slaughter one another; remember these words of mine!" After he had finished, he disappeared.[70]

It is equally eerie that the Buddha himself prophesied the end of Buddhism in India. Bu Ston, the Tibetan scholar, has cited *Chandragarbha-pariprichha*, in which the Buddha said:

---

[70]Li, Hwui, *The Life of Hiuen-tsiang*, Samuel Beal (trans.), Kegan Paul Trench Trubner and Company Limited, London, 1914, p. 150.

After I have passed away, during 500 years, a great number of living beings is to appear, who will act according to my Doctrine and obtain deliverance. Thereafter, during 500 years, there will appear many who practice meditation. But the kings, ministers and the ordinary living beings who were devoted to the Doctrine will subsequently become less in number. Thereupon, during another 500 years, a great number of teachers who expound the Highest Doctrine, and who lead the living beings to salvation will appear. The number of the Çrāvaka Arhats will however, become diminished. The kings and the greater part of the living beings will become mere hearers, but will not apply energy to realize (the precepts) and to live according to them. In such a way faith will become weakened. The protectors of the Highest Doctrine will grow distressed, and those who are not devoted to the Highest Doctrine will become more powerful than before. The kings of Jambudvipa will invade each other with war and disturbances will arise. When 300 years of these 500 will have passed away, the gods and Nāgas who live according to the Doctrine will no more exist, and the living beings will cease to believe in the Highest Doctrine.[71]

The Twilight Years

Between 1234 and 1236 CE, when Dharmasvamin visited Magadha, he found Nalanda still functioning, although deserted and damaged. He lived there for six months, gave a vivid eyewitness account, and reported that Nalanda had 'seven great (lofty) pinnacles in its centre, two had been erected by the Rājā and two by two great Acharyas, one each. On the outside, towards the North, stood fourteen lofty pinnacles (Śikharas). Outside of it, there were about

---

[71]Ston, Bu, *The History of Buddhism in India and Tibet*, E. Obermiller (trans.), Sri Satguru Publications, Delhi, 1999, p. 172.

eighty small Vihāras called a-ri-kha. Most of these were built by the Rājā. Some were built by the queen. They were damaged by the Turushkas, and there was absolutely no one to look after them, or to make offering. They were built of bricks and many were left undamaged.[72] Only two viharas, called Dha-na-ba and Ghu-na-ba, were in serviceable condition. The boundary of the mahavihara still existed, and its eastern and western gates were decorated with paintings of Tara, the Buddhist goddess of compassion who liberates people from their suffering, and other deities.

Dharmasvamin says that Nalanda's partial survival was due to certain superstitions among the soldiers. In one of the early expeditions, the Turks destroyed the temple of Jnananath within the precincts of Nalanda. They carried away its stones to Odantapuri for the construction of a mosque. They desecrated the image by throwing filth on it, and one of the soldiers who took part in the desecration died of colic pains in Odantapuri that evening. This incident dissuaded the Turushka soldiers from attacking Nalanda for a while.

In the summer of 1235 CE, Nalanda was again invaded by the Turks of Odantapuri, who arrested Jayadeva. In prison, he learnt that the Turks were planning another attack on Nalanda and managed to send a message to Rahulshribhadra. Consequently, all 70 disciples deserted him, but Dharmasvamin refused to leave him. He carried him on his back, and the two took refuge in the temple of Jnananath in whose miraculous powers they had implicit faith. When the 300 Turushka soldiers arrived, they could not trace Dharmasvamin and his guru. Hence, they may have returned after some vandalism. It is unclear whether Dharmasvamin completed his study at the temple of Jnananath or whether the acharya and his disciple returned to the monastery.

---

[72]*Biography of Dharmasvamin, A Tibetan Monk Pilgrim*, George Roerich (trans.), K.P. Jayaswal Research Institute, Patna, 1959, p. 90.

Roerich's assertion about the partial survival of Nalanda may be correct, as the Nalanda complex may have been too large to be destroyed in a single attack. Moreover, most structures were built of fire-burnt bricks, not stones required for mosques, so the vandalization may have been less. Nalanda, unlike Vikramshila, was not situated on the highway connecting the Ganga-Yamuna rivers. Having plundered it in his earlier raids, Khilji may not have felt it necessary to leave the main route connecting the two rivers.

The Tibetan account states that about a century later, Chingal Raja became very powerful in Bengal and brought all Hindus and Turushkas right up to Delhi under his control. Taranath mentions that Chingal Raja was originally a devotee of Brahmins. Still, under the influence of his queen, he embraced Buddhism. He made lavish offerings in Vajrasana by renovating all the temples and building the upper four storeys of the nine-storey temple destroyed by the Turushkas. He also made lavish offerings to the temple of Nalanda but did not build big centres for the doctrine there.

The Final Exodus

According to Taranath, with the destruction of the viharas by the Turushkas and the decline of Buddhism, the great monk scholars fled. Pandit Shakyashri of Kashmir went to Jagaddala, where he spent three years, and then to Tibet. The great Ratnarakshita from Vaishali went to Nepal. The great Pandit Jnanakargupta and a hundred minor pandits went to the southwest of India. The great scholar, Buddhashrimitra, Dashabala's disciple, Vajrashri, and many minor pandits fled far to the south. Sixteen remaining *mahant*s, including the scholars Sanghamashrijnana, Ravishribhadra and Chandrakaragupta, along with 200 minor pandits, went far to the east to Pu-khan, Mu-nan, Kamboja, and other places. Thus, by the end of the twelfth century, Buddhism and the great viharas in Magadha had almost become extinct.

Afterword

Nalanda continues to exert its magnetic pull. It still inspires the setting up of institutions in its name in different parts of the world. In India, the Nava Nalanda Mahavihara was set up in the afterglow of the independence movement. The venerable bhikku Jagdish Kashyap, who studied Pali and Buddhism in Sri Lanka and had taken upon himself the monumental task of reviving Buddhist learning in India, started teaching Pali and Buddhism in the Department of Sanskrit at the Banaras Hindu University, Varanasi. He soon shifted his activities to Nalanda in Bihar. During a visit to Myanmar, he was included in the entourage of the first President of India, Dr Rajendra Prasad. Overwhelmed by the rousing reception and respect with which the venerable Kashyap was received there, Dr Rajendra Prasad declared that the ancient seat of learning in Nalanda would be revived. Thus, in 1951, the Nava Nalanda Mahavihara came into existence, with the venerable Jagdish Kashyap as its founder-director. Since then, it has had its ups and downs but is now recognized as a deemed university. It has made a rich contribution to the field of Buddhist studies.

However, all the institutions that have been inspired by Nalanda are dedicated to Buddhist studies. Once again, 55 years after Dr Rajendra Prasad, the eleventh President of India Dr A.P.J. Abdul Kalam tried to revive Nalanda, as he said in a speech in the Bihar Assembly. He, too, wanted the university to have a strong Buddhist department and for the spirit of Buddhism to infuse every aspect of the university.

The Nava Nalanda Mahavihara already existed and could have been strengthened further. The outcome of the speech, however, was a daring step by the Government of India—the establishment of a Nalanda University in Rajgir in 2010 through the Nalanda University Act. Its vision was to be 'an international institution for the pursuit of intellectual, historical and spiritual studies.' It has been designated as an institution of national importance since its inception. This university is to contain a memory of the ancient Nalanda. It is premised on the shared intent of the member states of the East Asia Summit to rediscover and strengthen 'educational cooperation by tapping the East Asia Region's centres of excellence in education [...] (and) to improve understanding and appreciation of one another's heritage and history.' The vision statement further states that the aim is to seek and recover the lost connections and partnerships in the Asian region, as these go deep into the past and are reflected in many standard cultural features. The university is to provide a creative space that will be a centre of inter-civilizational dialogue for future generations.

The Challenges

This is a tall order for the university. It is a mixture of foreign policy, the revival of ancient learning and links. Can it be done by combining it with modern education, which has a futuristic outlook? Asia is a strife-ridden region with different countries at different levels of development. These countries have their interests in the polity of nations, and although a shared culture and spiritual heritage is valuable, many have moved on from it. Building pan-Asian links is perhaps more of a foreign policy agenda than that of the university's. It is a political aspiration which requires cooperation at the highest level. A university can only supplement it through its curriculum and teaching, not lead it. That depends on the governments concerned, as they are the decision-makers. An educational institution may have this as the cornerstone of its philosophy. Still, once established, it begins to have a grammar of its own based on the research interests and opportunities that the teachers have. They are autonomous, and a political diktat cannot be imposed on them because knowledge knows no boundaries. In the age of the internet and connectivity, collaborations can be established virtually. Also, universities are inherently keen to develop knowledge partnerships with every corner of the world and welcome students and teachers from anywhere without geopolitical considerations. The Nalanda Mahavihara also welcomed students from wherever they came and incorporated knowledge from different parts of the world which was appropriate to its basic aim. Since it was an institution devoted to Buddhist learning, it was easy to accept only certain types of scholars, teachers and students.

Education today privileges science and technology, which are at the forefront of research throughout the world. It affects the environment, medicine, agriculture, industry, livelihood, and other fields—every facet of our lives. Of course, it must be infused with spiritualism and ethics if we are not to destroy ourselves. Who would know this better than Dr A.P.J. Abdul Kalam himself? However, this needs to be built into the vision statement of Nalanda University. If the university succeeds in creating an alternative discourse to the prevailing one through pan-Asian linkages and collaborations, it will render pioneering service to both India and the world. Alternative visions of growth and development will begin to emerge. The only question is whether this is possible in the university at this stage. The university's mission statement appears rather vague. It needs to be sharper and better defined, as all academic structures would have to be developed around it. If the university aspires to work towards achieving the vision statement, in what timeframe can this be accomplished, considering this is bound to be a long and arduous process?

It is important to learn the lessons from ancient Nalanda from which the present university seeks to draw inspiration.

These will indicate what it takes to establish a university of excellence like the Nalanda Mahavihara. One needs to look at the location of the institution, the ethos of the place, the infrastructure of both the surrounding area and the mahavihara itself, the faculty and students and their relationship with each other, the rigour of the curriculum and teaching-learning processes, the library and resources available, and the support it received without interference in its functioning. It is also important to remember why the mahavihara lost its sheen even before it was finally destroyed.

Comparison of the Ancient and Modern

Shakraditya established the mahavihara in a prosperous village on a major trade route that passed through the nearby city of Rajagriha, the capital of Magadha, a powerful kingdom of Asia. The Tirthankara Mahavira spent 14 rain retreats here, lecturing and discoursing, and the Buddha himself gave discourses in the Pavarika mango grove. In effect, it was a vibrant centre of social and religious learning, easily accessible from Rajagriha and Pataliputra. Times have changed, and with it, Rajgir and Patna, the erstwhile Rajagriha and Pataliputra. While seeds, once planted, never die, there are over 800 years of overlay. The connectivity between Patna and Rajgir leaves a lot to be desired. Today's faculty and students look for easy access by air or train. The nearest airport for Rajgir is Patna, after which it is a two- to three-hour journey by road, which could do with some upgrades. Further, unlike in the past, Rajgir offers very little by way of the infrastructure expected of a town—medical aid, educational facilities, job opportunities, or recreational outlets—making it difficult to attract students and teachers.

Teachers and students are important. After all, a university is all about the interaction between teachers and students. While there are many lessons to be learnt from what made Nalanda excel as a centre of learning, one of the most important is the honesty and integrity of purpose, on the part of both teachers and students, together with their willingness to endure any hardship that came their way in their pursuit of knowledge. Nalanda had a galaxy of great teachers whose seminal works are studied to this day and will be studied forever. The fame of the mahavihara rested on these well-known acharyas. Any modern university today is known for its teachers and students, intellectual work, and the dissemination of the knowledge created. It is a place where not only knowledge is created but also new ground is broken and where constant striving for excellence exists. This was achieved in the ancient mahavihara through a culture of strict discipline, rigorous intellectual work and the ability to accept and answer academic challenges posed through debate and discussion. Universities in modern India can only dream of this kind of framework. Times have changed and it is impossible to recreate this ethos in today's universities. It would be an anachronism in any case. After all, in the mahavihara, all teachers and students were primarily monks who followed the path laid down by the Buddha. Even the lay students who studied at the mahavihara had to follow the discipline of these monks during their stay.

The mahavihara was supported by a galaxy of kings, who honoured the scholars and supported the university even when their fortunes were uncertain. This shows a commitment at the highest level to teaching and learning. They made an infrastructure that was spectacular in its beauty. At the modern, government-supported Nalanda University, even a decade past, the basic infrastructure was still in the process of being built. It might have been better for an institution of national importance to start with some basic infrastructure, like an academic block, an administrative block, a library, a guesthouse, and some residential facilities, which could have been expanded further as the university grew. It is difficult for a university to take off without a dedicated campus. Ideally, Rajgir itself needs to be developed as a university town, which would not only make the university grow but also help the region prosper. It is important to remember that the Nalanda Mahavihara declined even before its destruction. It declined when Buddhism declined in society, so its connection with the people became weak. Also, it became the seat of esoteric learning, which had no relationship with alleviating people's suffering—the cornerstone of Buddhism. It declined when the Pala kings, unlike the Guptas and the Vardhanas, did not grant autonomy to the mahavihara and started to control its functioning. They created rival institutions and began distributing resources among them. They promoted esoteric learning, reducing the rigorous intellectual culture of Nalanda to a cult with their own people at the helm of affairs. The headship of the mahavihara was meant for renowned scholars such as Dharmapala and Shilabhadra. When the Pala kings started putting their people as the heads of the institution, it suffered.

The lesson to be learnt from its decline is that universities must connect with society and the people. They must serve the society in which they are embedded, and they can do this through research that can be applied to ameliorate the lives of the people around them. Former President Abdul Kalam, a scientist deeply embedded in Indian traditions, must have wanted the traditions of excellence to be embedded in Nalanda, together with a futuristic scientific outlook. He would have wanted the university to build on the strengths of Asia and not exclude others. By reviving Nalanda, he must have wanted the scholars and all the processes of the university to be imbued with a spiritual and ethical outlook. If ideas never die, then perhaps the spirit of the mahavihara will take root in the new Nalanda University, and maybe Dr Kalam's ideas will one day come to fruition. However, a lot of honest soul-searching and hard work must be done for that to happen.

Select Reading

1. Cunningham, Alexander, *The Ancient Geography of India*, Low Price Publications, Delhi, 2006.
2. Sharma, Archana, 'The Nalanda Copperplate of Devapaladeva', *The Heritage of Nalanda*, in C. Mani (ed.), Aryan Books International, 1972.
3. Chatterjee, Arpita, 'Management of Nalanda Mahavira from Epigraphic Material', in C. Mani (ed.), *The Heritage of Nalanda*, Aryan Books International, 2008.
4. Waley, Arthur, *The Real Tripitaka and Other Pieces*, Routledge, 2011.
5. Stein, Aurel, *On Ancient Central Asian Tracks: Brief Narrative of Three Expeditions in Innermost Asua and Northwestern China*, Gyan Publishing House, 2021.
6. Barua, Benimadhab, *Gaya and Buddha Gaya Volume 1*, Legare Street Press, United Kingdom, 2022.
7. Sahai, Bhagwant, *The Inscriptions of Bihar*, Ramanand Vidya Bhawan, 1983.
8. *Biography of Dharasvamin: A Tibetan Monk Pilgrim*, Dr George Roerich (trans.), K.P. Jayaswal Research Institute, Patna, 1959.
9. Bu-ston, *The History of Buddhism in India and Tibet*, E. Obermiller (trans.), University of Heidelberg, 1932.
10. *The Heritage of Nalanda*, Mani, C., (ed.), Aryan Books International, Delhi, 2008.
11. Prasad, Chandra S., *Nalanda Its Mahaviharra and Xuan Zang*, Eastern Book Linkers, Delhi, 2016.
12. Prasad, Shekhar Chandra, 'Nalanda vis-à-vis the Birthplace of Śāriputra', *East and West*, Vol. 38, No. 1/4, 1988, pp. 175–188.
13. Charles River Editors, *The History and Legacy of the Trade Routes that Connected Europe and Asia*, 2016.
14. Thubron, Colin, *Shadow of the Silk Road*, Vintage, 2007.
15. Singh, Anuradha, 'Buddhism in Sarnath: An Account of Two Chinese Travellers', *Space and Culture*, Vol. 2, No. 2, 2014.
16. Benetti, Fernando J., 'A Historiographical review on Nālandā Mahāvihāra: Chinese, Persian, Archaeological sources and the role of "Nālandā tradition"

of Tibetan Buddhism', 2018, Nalanda University, Rajgir, MA dissertation.

17. Asher, Fredrick M., *Nalanda: Situating the Great Monastery*, Marg Foundation, 2015.

18. Lama, G.K., *The Art Heritage of Nalanda*, Buddhist World Press, Delhi, 2018.

19. Sankalia, Hasmukh D., *The University of Nalanda*, B.G. Paul & Co Publishers, Madras, 1934.

20. I Ching, *Chinese Monks in India: Biography of Eminent Monks who went to the Western World in Search of the Law during the Great T'and Dynasty*, Latika Lahiri (trans.), Motilal Banarsidass, Delhi, 2015.

21. I-Tsing, *A Record of Buddhist Religion as Practiced in India and Malay Archipelago, AD 671–695*, J. Takakusu (trans.), Oxford Calendron Press, 1998.

22. Shinohara, Koichi, 'Biographies of Eminent Monks in a Comparative Perspective: The Function of the Holy in Medieval Chinese Buddism', *Chung-Hwa Buddhist Journal*, No. 7, 1994, pp. 479–498.

23. Shinohara, Koichi, 'Evolution of Chan Biographies of Eminent Monks', *Bulletin de l'École française d'Extrême-Orient*, Vol. 85, 1998, pp. 306–324.

24. Saran, Mishi, *Chasing the Monk's Shadow*, Penguin India, Delhi, 2008.

25. Monk Hui-Li, *The Life of Hsuan-Tsang: The Tripitaka-Master of the Great Tzu En Monastery*, Li Yung-His (trans.), Samyak Prakashan, Delhi, 2023.

26. Majumdar, N.G., *Monographs of the Varendra Research Society, Nalanda Copperplate of Devapaladeva*, Museum of the Varendra Research Society, Calcutta, 1926.

27. Sastri, Hirananda, *Nalanda and its Epigraphic Material*, No. 66, Archaeological Survey of India, New Delhi, 1942.

28. Dung, Nguyen Thi Phuon, 'The First Chinese Pilgrim Monk Went to India and Comparison with the Travelling of Hsuan Tsang', *International Journal of Science and Research*, Volume 8, Issue 6, 2019.

29. Bapat, P.V., *2500 Years of Buddhism*, The Publication Division, Ministry of Information and Broadcasting, Government of India, 1956.

30. 'Dhammacakkappavattana Sutta: Setting in Motion the Wheel of Truth', Access to Insight, https://tinyurl.com/bddtbftb. Accessed on 9 May 2025.

31. *Nalanda-Buddhism And The World Research Volume-VI*, Golden Jubilee Volume, R. Panth (ed.), Nava Nalanda Mahavihara, 2001.

32. Ranasinghe, R.H.I.S., 'The Memories of Chinese Buddhist Scholars in connection with Nalanda Monastic International University in India in the 7th century AD', 74th IFLA General Conference and Council, https://tinyurl.com/mr4awkfm Accessed on 19 June 2025.

33. Tagore, Rabindranath, *Talks in China*, Rupa Publications, New Delhi, 2002.

34. Singh, Rana P.B., 'Sacredness and Manescape: The Sacred Geography of Gaya, India,' *Facets of Social Geography: International and Indian Perspectives* Ashok K. Dutt, Vandana Wadhwa, Baleshwar Thakur and Frank J. Costa, (eds.), Cambridge University Press, 2012.

35. Wiggins, Sally Hovey, *The Silk Road Journey With Xuanzang*, Basic Books, 2003.

36. Shramana Yijing, *Buddist Monastic Traditions of Southern Asia: A Record of the Inner Law Sent Home From The South Seas*, Li Rongxi (trans.), Numata Center for Buddist Translation and Research, California, 2000.

37. Dutt, Sukumar, *Buddhist Monks and Monasteries: Their History and Their Contribution to Indian Culture*, Motilal Banarsidass, New Delhi, 2015.

38. Chung, Tan, *China: A 5,000-year Odyssey*, SAGE Publications, New Delhi, 2016.

39. Sen, Tansen, *India, China and the World: A Connected History*, Rowman and Littlefield, 2017.

40. Sen, Tansen, *Buddhism Across Asia: Networks of Material, Intellectual and Cultural Exchange*, Vol. 1, Institute of South Asian Studies, 2014.

41. 'Theravada Collection on Monastic Law: The Small Division: The Chapter on Minor Topics', Suttacentral.net, https://tinyurl.com/ta52j3a6. Accessed on 9 May 2025.

42. Lu, Yang, 'Narrative and Historicity in the Buddhist Biographies of Early Medieval China: The Case of Kumarajiva', *Asia Major Third Series*, Vol. 17, No. 2, 2004, pp. 1–43.

Index